T0331048

Track
to the Future

**Investment, Finance and
Lessons for the New Economy**

Track
to the *Future*

Investment, Finance and
Lessons for the New Economy

Joseph Cherian
Asia School of Business, Malaysia & Cornell University, USA

World Scientific

NEW JERSEY · LONDON · SINGAPORE · BEIJING · SHANGHAI · HONG KONG · TAIPEI · CHENNAI · TOKYO

Published by

World Scientific Publishing Co. Pte. Ltd.

5 Toh Tuck Link, Singapore 596224

USA office: 27 Warren Street, Suite 401-402, Hackensack, NJ 07601

UK office: 57 Shelton Street, Covent Garden, London WC2H 9HE

National Library Board, Singapore Cataloguing in Publication Data
Name(s): Cherian, Joseph.
Title: Track to the future : investment, finance and lessons for the new economy /
    Joseph Cherian.
Description: Singapore : World Scientific Publishing Co. Pte. Ltd., [2023]
Identifier(s): ISBN 978-981-12-6192-3 (hardback) | ISBN 978-981-12-6193-0
    (ebook for institutions) | ISBN 978-981-12-6194-7 (ebook for individuals)
Subject(s): LCSH: Finance. | Investments. | Economics.
Classification: DDC 332--dc23

British Library Cataloguing-in-Publication Data
A catalogue record for this book is available from the British Library.

For any available supplementary material, please visit
https://www.worldscientific.com/worldscibooks/10.1142/13014#t=suppl

Desk Editor: Nicole Ong

Typeset by Stallion Press
Email: enquiries@stallionpress.com

Printed in Singapore

Acknowledgements

Firstly, I must thank my dear wife, Emma Yanfang Cherian, who was the first member of my immediate family to end up in the financial (asset management) industry in the 1990s, and who influenced me greatly to embark on my professional career trajectory that bridges theory and practice, and who was also a co-author to many of my articles, some of which are reproduced here. She serves as a constant inspiration, constructive critique, and — as a certified sailor, scuba diver, and polyglot — the most interesting member (and risk-taker) of the family!

Secondly, I must thank all the professors, teachers, mentors, and/or co-authors who have greatly influenced my (evolving) thinking to date: Professors Zvi Bodie, Robert Jarrow, Marti Subrahmanyam, Bernard Yeung, and Robert Merton (of *Mertonian Finance* fame). Their adherence to the scientific method of enquiry in all things considered is admirable. It is not an exaggeration to emphatically state that *Mertonian Finance* is what influenced many of us in our professional careers in this field.

Thirdly, I am grateful to all my co-authors over the years, some of whom I have already mentioned above. The others include Christine Kon, Li Ziyun, Ranjan Chakravarty, Laurent Lassalvy, Yougesh Khatri, Manish Sansi, Katrina Cokeng, Danny Yong, Ong Shien Jin, Johnson Jingyuan Mo, Xiao Tingyi, William Weng, Lee Kang Hoe, Michel Alexandre Cardin, Nishimura Kiyoshi, Wong Heang Fine, Ang Swee Hoon, and Jack Loo.

I would be remiss not to thank my friends at World Scientific Publishing, particularly this book's editor, Nicole Ong Shi Min, for her constant encouragement and overall editorial supervision of the book, and assistant director Angela Dong Lixi, who was not only a former MBA student of mine at NUS Business School but also the behind-the-scenes cheerleader of this book.

Finally, to my personal copyeditor and proofreader, the one and only Paul StJohn Mackintosh of Geneva, whose copious attention to detail and critical feedback made this book as polished as it currently is.

I hope I have not missed thanking anyone. And if I have, my eternal apologies for the unintentional oversight!

About the Author

Joseph Cherian is Practice Professor of Finance, Asia School of Business and Cornell University (Visiting). He was the former Practice Professor of Finance at the National University of Singapore (NUS). Prior to NUS, Joe was Managing Director, Global Head and CIO of the Quantitative Strategies Group at Credit Suisse in New York where he had direct responsibility for over US$67 billion in client assets managed to a quantitative discipline. While at Credit Suisse, Joe served on the Global Executive Committee, as well as various senior management, investments, and risk committees of the Asset Management division. He joined the financial industry in New York after an academic career in the US, including as an Associate Professor of Finance at Boston University. He was formerly an Executive-in-Residence and a two-term member of the Johnson Graduate School of Management's Dean's Advisory Council at Cornell University and is now an Emeritus Member of the Dean's Council. Joe currently serves as an Advisor to Xen Capital, a boutique global digital wealth and alternatives asset manager in Singapore, Singapore Exchange (SGX), Asia Asset Management in Hong Kong, as well as the Mercer-CFA Institute Global Pensions Index's Advisory Board in Australia. He has had appointments at Singapore's Central Provident Fund (CPF) Advisory Panel and the National Research Foundation's Early-Stage Venture Fund Evaluation Panel. He was an Independent Non-Executive Director of Bursa Malaysia in Kuala Lumpur, a Scientific Advisor to Nipun Capital, a boutique hedge fund based in San Francisco, a scientific consultant to Fullerton Fund Management, a Temasek subsidiary in Singapore, and on the *Journal of Alternative Investments*' Editorial Board in the US. Joe holds a BSc in Electrical Engineering from MIT, and MSc and PhD degrees in Finance from Cornell University.

Preface

In an edited collection of past writings, op-eds, commentaries, and essays that covers translational research, objective finance theory and investment science, personal observations, and hands-on practical advice from an academic-practitioner's unique career in both academia and the finance industry, this volume contributes to the body of knowledge in areas of finance as wide ranging as asset management, lifecycle savings, investing, infrastructure finance, digital currency, disruption in the new economy, macroeconomic applications in capital markets, debt, and the sustainable and political economy. The practical suggestions and personal insights included could prove useful — and serve as a resource — to professionals, retail and institutional investors, policymakers, regulators, finance practitioners, and academics, both research-track and clinical, who are interested in the practice of modern finance theory.

Introduction

I started my professional life off as an engineer — an electrical engineer. It meant putting theoretical knowledge into practice, building engineering systems and processes (sometimes from scratch), and making dynamic adjustments along the way as obstacles, problems, and challenges presented themselves during the implementation of such systems.

In a way, my engineering experience, and *best-in-class* training prior to that, prepared me for the next inflexion point in my professional journey. I went on to complete my graduate studies in financial engineering at another *best-in-class* institution. It prepared me for my career in academics initially (in Boston), and then Wall Street, and finally shifting gears to become a practice (a.k.a. clinical) professor in finance in Singapore. Throughout my "second" career, I always found the bridge between theory and practice the most fascinating. This was probably because Boston in the 1990s was also the capital of the asset management industry, which meant billions of dollars in retirement assets were also managed in Boston by financial institutions that were both behemoths and household names, such as Fidelity Investments, State Street Global Advisors, Wellington Management, Putnam Investments, and John Hancock Investment Management. There was hence a bit of an asset management rub-off effect on me when it came to my research and interests!

My initial research in finance involved the pricing and hedging of derivative securities, fixed income instruments such as bonds, financial market liquidity, and market manipulation. These areas of research were influenced largely by two academic greats in our field who had a huge interest in practice — my Ph.D. dissertation advisor and frequent co-author, Professor Robert A. Jarrow of Cornell University's Johnson Graduate School Management, and my other frequent co-author, Professor Marti Subrahmanyam of NYU-Stern.

I then began to develop an interest in retirement finance, driven mainly by one of the greatest pension thinkers, translational researchers, and investments scientists I know, Professor (Emeritus) Zvi Bodie of Boston University School of Management, who describes his strand of active research as *Mertonian Finance*, aptly named after his colleague, co-author, and the Nobel laureate, Professor Robert C. Merton of MIT-Sloan. I have been greatly influenced by this strand of pension research. My first foray into Treasury Inflation-Protected Securities (TIPS) and Savings I-Bonds in the late 90s was a result of the numerous lunch and off-lunch discussions I had with these two financial greats. With inflation running at 7.9 percent per annum (y-o-y) in February 2022, after a long spell of declining interest rates and inflation (both have been on the decline in the major economies since the early 1980s), suddenly, their advice to me that you don't avoid buying car insurance just because the accident rate in your neighbourhood is low currently began to make eminent sense! Investing in a safety net, laddered portfolio of inflation-linked bonds on personal account since the late 1990s has been one of my best investments to date.

I then moved to Wall Street while on sabbatical leave — and never went back to teaching — which is also where I developed my keen interest in research being put into practice. I began to have a greater appreciation of the impact systematic investing, good risk management, high fees, and high sales loads had on risk-adjusted performance, on fiduciary responsibility, and so on. And I began writing on those topics.

When I moved back to Asia in the late 2000s for family reasons (the ageing population syndrome was hitting my own home!), I re-joined the academy as a practice professor, where bridging finance theory and practice was the core mission and stated mandate, which is what professional schools in medicine, law, and business are or should be all about. Given the natural evolution of interests influenced by economic innovations and transformations, and the nature of the problems and challenges faced by countries in this region, my translational finance research also began to evolve. I started studying and writing in areas as far-flung as infrastructure finance, digital currency, disruption in the new economy, macroeconomic applications in capital markets, debt, and the sustainable and political economy. This was in addition to my usual research in asset management, lifecycle savings, investing, hedge funds, market liquidity, market manipulation, and so on.

I have tried to compile a collection of all my past single-authored and co-authored writings on these topics, re-writing them in an easy-to-read manner for both hard-core finance academics as well as professionals, retail and institutional investors, policymakers, regulators, and finance practitioners who are interested in the practice of modern finance theory.

Just a special word on the use of currency in the text. Since currencies fluctuate, I have provided most of the currency references in local currency terms, for example, the U.S. dollar (US$), Singapore dollar (S$), Australian dollar (A$), and Malaysian ringgit (RM). It will also depend on the context, where I could default to the U.S. dollar if it conveys the message better.

I also refer to my published articles in the third person, for example, as "Cherian (2021)" or "Cherian and Yan (2019)". This is for the convenience of exposition and completeness — it allows the reader to go back to the source article directly, which is available in the Reference section at the end.

I hope you enjoy reading this collection of essays as much as I enjoyed writing it!

Contents

Acknowledgements   v

About the Author   vii

Preface   ix

Introduction   xi

Part 1   **Asset Management, Lifecycle Savings, and Investing**   1

Chapter 1   On the Role of the State in Retirement Savings   3

Chapter 2   Retirement Savings — The Seven Pillars   22

Chapter 3   Making a Good Programme Even Better   32

Chapter 4   A Word on (Retirement Savings) Costs and Longevity   37

Chapter 5   A Vignette on the State of the Asset Management
              Industry   42

Chapter 6   Making Promises We Can't Keep: The Asian Pensions
              Predicament   49

Chapter 7   Terms of Endurement: Retirement Solutions Should
              Harness Investment Science and Technology to
              Shockproof Plans   54

Chapter 8   Algo's Got Rhythm   60

Chapter 9   Are Hedge Funds Just Traditional Beta?   66

Chapter 10   In Bonds We (Still) Trust   76

Chapter 11   In Bonds We (Still) Trust: Part 2   83

Part 2   **Infrastructure Finance, Digital Currency,**
                    Disruption, and New Economy   **91**

Chapter 12   Making Infrastructure Assets More Palatable: A Unified
             Market Approach to Infrastructure Financing   93

Chapter 13   Infrastructure Financing   99

Chapter 14   Oh, Behave! Why the AIIB Can Be a Win for China
             and Asia: Can China Bring Its Mojo to the World of
             Infrastructure Financing?   103

Chapter 15   On the Role of Blockchain in Democratizing the
             Investment Opportunity Set   107

Chapter 16   The Long March to the Future Economy   112

Part 3   **Macro, Debt, Sustainable, and Political Economy**   **117**

Chapter 17   SME Financing: The Need for Out-of-the-Box
             Thinking for the Next Systemic Crisis   119

Chapter 18   Additional Safeguards for India's Growth Prospects:
             A Macro-finance Perspective   128

Chapter 19   Hazenomics: Facing the Fire   135

Chapter 20   The State As Insurer of Last Resort   140

Chapter 21   Financial Trade-Offs Matter during Pandemics   147

Chapter 22   A Turning Point Moment of Interest (or Why Is
             Everyone Afraid of Inflation?)   154

Chapter 23   China's Big-Tech Crackdown and Financial Markets:
             Investors Aren't As Afraid As You Might Think   168

Chapter 24   The Swan Song March? An Update on China's Big
             Tech Crackdown   173

References   181

Part 1

Asset Management, Lifecycle Savings, and Investing

On the Role of the State in Retirement Savings

My interest in retirement savings commenced in academia with valuation issues — be they in the pricing or hedging of derivatives, equities, bonds, etc. It slowly developed into exploring more in-depth issues pertaining to lifecycle savings and investing. This includes the decumulation (or spending) phase of our retirement years.

My years spent in academia, and subsequently in the financial industry — managing primarily institutional client assets — brought home to me the importance of the state in all things retirement. This is where my explorations began into the linkages between lifecycle savings and investing, the state, the asset management industry, and the asset owners involved, particularly the pension and retirement savings entities, such as the U.S.'s 401(k)s, Malaysia's Employee Provident Fund (EPF), Singapore's Central Provident Fund (CPF), and Hong Kong's Mandatory Provident Fund (MPF).

In my first post-industry article discussing the role of the state in the pension system (Cherian and Lassalvy, 2011), my co-author and I address two fundamental questions[1]:

1. What is the role of the state in a retirement savings system?
2. How to set about fulfilling that role efficiently?

---

[1] Many of the ideas in this part of the exposition are also based on Lassalvy (2011) when he was a Senior Research Fellow at the Center for Asset Management Research & Investments (CAMRI) at NUS Business School.

1.1 Introduction

A pension system's primary objective should be to guarantee some form of stable standard of living (i.e., indexed to inflation) in retirement. It could be a hybrid public–private pension system. However, the public pension system should have the primary responsibility of delivering a basic pension to all, given the long-term nature of the obligation, and the need for reliability, some form of guarantee, security, and trust.

To provide for the cost-of-living adjustment, there need to be fixed-income securities whose cash flows can reasonably track the standard of living. In the U.S. there are inflation-indexed government bonds called Treasury Inflation-Protected Securities (TIPS), which allow for cost-of-living indexation. Unfortunately, Asia Pacific governments, except for a few — like Australia and Japan — do not offer such inflation hedging instruments.

In the closing segment, we provide a few thoughts on the retirement saver's contribution (or accumulation) phase, as part of the lifecycle savings, as well as addressing real estate needs and healthcare costs.

1.2 Ensuring a Dignified Standard of Living in Retirement

The key retirement income concern for the average citizen is that she receives a reasonable payment every month, which lasts for as long as she lives, and which is indexed to her standard of living. Pension research usually focuses on cost of living, but the first-best benchmark is probably the standard of living, as measured by changes in per capita consumption. The latter is about enabling individuals to purchase the same percentage of per capita consumption as the standard of living rises. It is commonly referred to as "keeping up with the Joneses". Nobel laureate Robert C. Merton (1983) demonstrates that standard-of-living (or consumption) indexing is desirable, sustainable, macro-consistent, and allows for citizens' risk sharing in the real economy, as measured by aggregate consumption. His main argument in favour of consumption indexing is that inflation adjustment alone would not be able to maintain one's relative standard of living. Consumption indexing helps mitigate the divergence between the quality of life of retirees and that of the working population. That said, a cost-of-living adjustment, as provided by TIPS in the case of the U.S., is still a reasonable second-best benchmark versus no indexation at all.

Why standard of living over cost of living? If prices remain constant over a certain period but quantities consumed double, the cost of living is unchanged while the standard of living has doubled. As such, pension distributions which track cost of living could result in significant divergences over time between the quality of life of retirees and the working population — and perhaps disappointment for the retirees.

In summary, maintaining the individual's standard of living on a relative basis could be attempted through consumption-indexed life annuities, measurement complexities and errors notwithstanding. These instruments currently do not exist. If they did, a first pass-through proxy measure of aggregate per capita consumption could be calculated using VAT or GST receipts, which are paid by consumers. Merton (1983) had suggested calculating each person's consumption as the residual in a cash flow analysis. In his proposed pension system, contributions are based on everyone's consumption, requiring measurement of individual consumption. Practically speaking, individual consumption could be calculated as the difference between the annual flow of disposable income and savings.

1.3 A Hybrid Approach: Coexistence of Public and Private Retirement Systems

Many developed and some developing countries, particularly in Asia, are experiencing not just rising life expectancy but declining fertility as well. This population ageing problem reduces the support ratio, i.e., the ratio of the active working population (usually defined as people aged 15–64) to non-working retirees (defined as 65 and above). Therefore, the sustainability of pay-as-you-go pension or social security "savings" systems, where current retirees' pensions are financed by current workers, is very much in doubt — unless the national debt, already under strain due to pandemic-related financial support packages, is increased to even more unsustainable levels.

In private defined contribution plans, there are concerns about the future value of each person's retirement fund, given that the investment risk during the accumulation phase is transferred from financial institutions (or producers) to consumers. Additionally, consumers' ability to convert the (uncertain) accumulated funds into a reasonable retirement income for life, appropriately indexed, at the point of retirement, is both a shaky and expensive proposition.

Given the economic and political complexity of implementing radical adjustments to an existing pension system, most adjustments are in practice made at the margins. For example, pension experts correctly recommend raising the retirement age or the contribution amount, reducing discretionary retirement expenses, monetizing equity in one's home via a reverse mortgage, etc. These suggestions, which I have also made in various fora, only help alleviate — and not eliminate — the problems of retirement savings underfunding and lack of financial literacy. Reforming the fundamental structure of the retirement savings system, be it public, private, or hybrid, is more important, yet seldom debated.

In a nutshell, Cherian and Lassalvy (2011) and Lassalvy (2011) have the view that the state should aim to guarantee all citizens a basic living pension that is indexed to the standard of living, while additional pension savings and retirement income should be left to a well-intentioned and well-trained private sector.[2] By that, we mean that the financial sector providing such retirement services should be acting in a more responsible and fiduciary manner when it comes to retirement assets. The corollary to that is that they (1) deliver services at the lowest feasible cost and (2) are held to a higher fiduciary standard by the financial regulators!

A person's well-being is affected by the living conditions of people around them. While the aforementioned "keeping up with the Joneses" argument justifies the standard-of-living adjustment in retirement payouts, people can also feel less happy if they see or know folks around them are starving or suffering unnecessarily. These externalities help explain why most countries have developed social welfare nets to help the

---

[2] I owe a great debt to Laurent Lassalvy, whose many conversations with me, essays, and time spent at my previous base at NUS Business School (CAMRI) have influenced much of this chapter.

most deprived. It would be complex and costly for governments to support entire populations of resource-deprived retired senior citizens. So, there is both a need and a benefit for the state to mandate that their people save enough during their working lives, such that they are all entitled — in fact, guaranteed — to receive a dignified level of income throughout their retirement years. These externalities may not be considered in a pure free-market private pension system, leading to a condition referred to as "market incompleteness" by financial economists.

The main objective of the public pension system should be to guarantee a minimum — or better still, a dignified — standard of living for all its citizens. Two additional objectives of the public retirement system should be self-funding (distributions are paid from contributions) and self-reliance (each citizen's distribution in retirement is funded from his or her own past pension contribution).

At the point of retirement, consumption-linked — or at a minimum, inflation-linked — life annuities should be the compulsory baseline retirement investment product within the public pension system. This system should be by construction low cost, sustainable, trustworthy, and safe.

To fix ideas and provide real-world examples of the above exposition, I draw on two quick illustrations. One is based on Singapore's Central Provident Fund (CPF) experience, and the other from the U.S. private insurance sector's life annuity quotes. The CPF LIFE Estimator calculates the expected life annuity payout from S$100,000 cumulated at age 65 to be between S$585 and S$616 per month for males.[3] Meanwhile, the U.S.'s *Annuity Shopper Buyer's Guide* in its Winter 2020 issue calculates a similar life annuity paid out by the U.S. insurance sector at about US$437 per month on average per US$100,000 saved.[4] The fairly big difference in monthly payouts could be driven by generous interest rates in the former case (the Singapore government subsidizes the CPF savings and life annuity interest rates), the private sector's high fees, differing population mortality tables, and so on.

---

[3] See CPF LIFE Estimator Calculator. URL: https://www.cpf.gov.sg/eSvc/Web/Schemes/LifeEstimator/LifeEstimator.

[4] See Annuity Shopper Buyer's Guide — ImmediateAnnuities.com (Winter 2020). URL: https://www.immediateannuities.com/annuity-shopper/.

To summarize, the above features, and the need to pool risks across cohorts, health profiles, mortality tables, and demographic factors, necessitate a mandatory system with no individual choice on offer for the baseline public pension or social security savings system.

The advantage of making deferred or immediate life annuities the compulsory retirement investment product is that it removes any *adverse selection* cost. Transforming cash into a life annuity is a great investment for people who will live much longer than their age group, and a bad investment for those who will live much shorter than their age group. As such, there is an incentive for the unhealthy who do not expect to live long to not subscribe to life annuities. If this indeed were an option, the overall population mortality tables would not be applicable to the calculation of the life annuity conversion factor, which would result in both lower annuities for each dollar contributed and an increase the uncertainty/risk for the provider of the life annuities — in our case, the state.

Another problem that can arise by not having mandatory baseline retirement savings and retirement annuity is the *free-rider* conundrum. This is when people don't save nearly enough to accumulate a sufficient basic sum at the point of retirement that can be annuitized into a subsistence income stream in retirement. They instead end up relying on various public safety nets, or as a ward of the state in retirement.

The basic compulsory public retirement system as described above allows for a decent and low-cost way of achieving a dignified income path for retirees. Everyone should be entitled and encouraged to save more during their working lives, to work longer, and to even monetize any real assets, such as the equity in their home, to receive a higher retirement income payout. Savvy workers should be encouraged to do all the above during their working lives in order to avoid a major drop in their standard of living during retirement.

However, any additional savings over and above the basic compulsory public retirement system, which usually involves government transfers and subsidies, should be entirely discretionary. The resulting investments should therefore be managed on a purely commercial basis by the private financial sector. This would send a clear signal that the state is only prepared to interfere in the public component of the retirement system — and that it will interfere in the private sector only when absolutely necessary, for example, when addressing significant externalities (e.g., systemic risks, widespread potential counterparty failures, or problematic fee structures), which may not potentially be accounted for in a pure free-market system.

The private sector should deliver more competition and a larger choice of products for savers/future retirees — and yet not so much choice that it leads to investor paralysis. It could also allow for the tailoring of future retirement distributions to individual desires. People would have the choice between subscribing to additional deferred consumption-linked annuities (public or private), investing the contributions in marketable securities (say, equities, fixed income, balanced funds, or target date funds), or any other financial product. There would be no government guarantee on such retirement assets, be they financial investments in the accumulation phase or life annuities in the decumulation years. Individuals would have to consider the risks associated in making such investments, including the long-term creditworthiness of the private pension provider, perhaps with the help of a professional financial advisor.

In parallel, private pension providers should be closely regulated to ensure prudent financial management. In addition to enacting regulations and laws, such as the ERISA in the U.S., the government can also have a strong influence on the private pension system through tax incentives, which encourage additional retirement savings and/or investments in low-risk life annuities.

1.4 Public Pension Retirement Income and Manufacturing Consumption-indexed Returns

I have argued that a good retirement savings system should see a government provide a baseline life annuity — be it inflation or consumption indexed — to its citizens, based on their past contributions and earned annuity credits. In this capacity, the government acts as a financial intermediary: It receives cash today from its citizens and promises annuity payments in a distant future and for an uncertain length of time (life annuities). How should the government approach these significant, distant, and uncertain financial obligations? And what is the responsibility of individuals regarding the level of contribution during the accumulation phase?

One possible approach is the "pay-as-you-go" system, where all individual pension contributions are allocated to the government's general budget, and pension obligations are only assumed when they become due — financing them through the general budget as with any other government expense. As Lassalvy (2011) argues, there are significant problems with this approach:

➢ Lack of accountability: the government receives revenues now and pays pensions later. This increases the chances of the government mismanaging its resources and over-spending during the early or good years.

➢ Significant demographic and economic risk. A pay-as-you-go system achieves self-funding through inter-generational transfers. As such, it is highly dependent on the evolution of the support ratio. Furthermore, without investing in consumption-linked fixed income products in an asset–liability management (ALM) framework, the government is heavily exposed to future inflation and standard-of-living growth, which are both highly uncertain.

➢ No market-based pricing check: Without a specific funding programme for future annuity liabilities — say, by the introduction of consumption-linked bonds and the construction of the associated consumption-linked yield curve — there would be no market-based determination of what one dollar today is worth in terms of a consumption-indexed life annuity a few decades from now. And by extension, it would not be possible to ensure individual self-reliance or the requisite financing level needed now to achieve the baseline annuity that maintains the individual's basic standard of living in retirement. Furthermore, the absence of external market checks increases the risk of political interference, be it in the determination of the annuity conversion factor, the calculation of the appropriate cost of living indices, etc.

A preferable approach would be to create a self-funded (but not entirely self-directed), government-guaranteed public pension or social security savings fund — and then create a financial environment which allows the pension fund to reduce as much as possible the uncertainties affecting its asset–liability management. Singapore's CPF is a case in point. Every time a member (or his/her employer) contributes (or matches) a dollar, the CPF channels that dollar to the Singapore government, which issues a Special Singapore Government Security (SSGS) to the CPF Board. In true asset–liability management fashion, these non-tradable government bonds not only pay a much higher set of interest rates to CPF members than traditional capital market bonds issued via Singapore Government Securities (SGS) but are also designed to meet the basic retirement needs of CPF members in a safe, sustainable, and adequate manner. CPF members have the option to invest any quantity above this basic amount, whether in more risky equity investments or insurance-linked products, via the CPF Investment Scheme (CPFIS).

As an aside, the monies raised from these SGS are commingled by the Singapore government with all other proceeds from government fundraising activities, like land sales, and handed over to the government's fund manager, Government of Singapore Investment Corporation Private Limited (GIC), to be managed for long-term total returns.

In order to enhance the accountability of the national retirement savings system, the government could establish an independent legal entity or a Board of Trustees with fiduciary responsibility to ensure proper accounting of individual pension contributions, prudent construction of the various savings schemes — be they asset–liability management, liability-driven investing, and/or plain old risky total returns programmes — and the ability to pay life annuities to pensioners in their retirement years.

Here are some safeguards to consider when designing a robust social security or pension savings scheme:

1. To reduce political interference or bias, the public pension fund should be responsible for setting (on a purely commercial but cost-effective basis) the annuity conversion factors applicable, and updating them whenever needed, preferably via an independent pension commission or advisory panel. The retirement obligations of this public pension fund (i.e., the pension annuities payments) would be formally guaranteed by the government up to a cap; this would remove any potential annuity

payout or counterparty risk concerns from contributors and assure them that their basic pension is guaranteed by the state.

2. The government should issue consumption-indexed savings bonds, indexed to the standard of living or inflation at a minimum, so that the public pension fund can purchase assets (real bonds) which closely match its liabilities (the average citizenry's real expenditures or spending). Aside from making consumption sufficiency unattainable in real dollars, the absence of consumption-indexed bonds would make it difficult for the public pension fund to price the annuity conversion factor, given the absence of comparables to work from. Plus, estimating or predicting distant future aggregate consumption levels is a highly complex endeavour, best left to capital markets. The government is also the most credible issuer of long-term consumption-linked bonds, as it can finance them through highly correlated funding activities, like via consumption taxes (e.g., VAT/ GST). This facility, along with the government's ability to introduce price controls, if necessary, is not available to the corporate sector. Hence, it is unreasonable to unload the burden onto the private financial or corporate sector. However, once the government has issued an entire term structure of such securities, even possibly out to 80 years, the private sector (comprising financial services firms) can innovate around the theme by offering consumption-linked financial and insurance products.

At this juncture, sceptics and some governments may question the ability of the government to issue consumption-indexed bonds. However, several developed countries have already been issuing inflation-adjusted bonds for many years (e.g., the U.S., Japan, France, Sweden, and Israel), but none have experimented with consumption-linked bonds. At the macro level, encouraging retirement savings above the basic public pension should help the economy, by increasing the savings rate and limiting the drop in standard of living during retirement.

Assuming that consumption-indexed government bonds are available at all maturities (e.g., up to 80 years), the only remaining risks faced by the public pension fund are the population's longevity risk and the government's credit risk. The recent turmoil in peripheral European sovereign debt demonstrates that the long-assumed risk-free status of most developed nations' sovereign bonds might have been an overly optimistic assumption. Nevertheless, except in a few specific cases, developed nations' government debt is still considered low risk and safer than corporate bonds, especially over a long horizon. Furthermore, national government sovereign risk will always be present in any pension system, including the U.S.'s federally run Social Security insurance programme, which provides basic retirement benefits to many Americans.

One issue that needs to be addressed at the national level is the insurance and hedging of longevity risk. This represents the risk that people live longer than expected, or as national mortality tables suggest. The sovereign is the natural provider of such longevity (a.k.a. tail risk) insurance, as it can do the following:

1. Mandate the automatic investments of compulsory public pension contributions.
2. Spread the risk of population longevity across the entire contributor pool.
3. Raise funds for this purpose on an ongoing basis, in case of shortfall, by means of taxation, land sales, adjustments to current contributions, etc.

Although it might be theoretically possible for a public pension fund to purchase longevity risk insurance from the private sector, say from insurance companies or banks, the benefits would be limited, because longevity risk would be replaced by counterparty risk and a non-negligible premium that would have to be paid, given the tail risks are not spread efficiently, but rather in pockets of private insurance pools or cohorts.

In summary, I have argued so far that the basic public retirement savings system that maintains the average retiree's standard of living should be operated through the following:

1. a self-funded independent public pension or social security savings fund,

2. whose obligations are guaranteed by the state,
3. where the government should issue consumption-indexed (or inflation-linked) bonds of all horizons for the public pension fund to invest in, and
4. in which cumulated funds at members' retirement should be converted into a consumption-indexed (or inflation-indexed) life annuity.

Anything over this basic pension savings system can certainly be privately managed, invested in risky assets and securities, etc. However, given the long-term nature of pension obligations, it must come with some amount of fiduciary oversight and regulatory supervision.

1.5 Working-life Contributions to the Public Pension Plan

I argued that it was optimal for the public pension plan to be compulsory and fully invested in consumption-indexed life annuities. The question is how much it should pay. Let us say we set it at 50 percent of the average per capita consumption from age 65 (or whatever the retirement age beyond that is). In the case of Singapore, that would work out to be around S$1,800 per month. This seems like a reasonable benchmark to target, as the bottom quintile of Singapore's households are documented to spend around S$2,600 per month, with the average household size at approximately 3.16 persons.

In this section, I will first discuss necessary public pension contributions and the influence of the annuity conversion factor, and then cover the specific cases of healthcare expenditures and real estate monetization.

All public pension contributions made during one's working life should be immediately converted into a consumption-indexed life annuity starting from a known date. The annuity conversion factor (from cash today to future life annuity) is therefore the key variable which will influence how much must be saved to achieve the 50 percent of per capita consumption life annuity objective. In an approach referred to as dynamic programming, Cherian and Ong (2020) propose to futureproof and shockproof retirement solutions by drawing on investment science, including stochastic dynamic programming, artificial intelligence, and big data analytics, to create a target income-focused private retirement plan that is personalized and customized over an investor's lifecycle. This "head start" lifecycle savings and investing approach could potentially be used to achieve the 50 percent of per capita consumption life annuity target.

On top of longevity risk, savers also face real interest rate risk. Indeed, the real interest rate on inflation-indexed bonds has never been lower in history: They are negative in many parts of the world, including the U.S., at the time of writing. The lower the real interest rates, the more expensive the bond. As a consequence, asset–liability management becomes a very expensive proposition, until interest rates normalize to their long-term average. There are indeed indications recently that this is the case. In 2022, interest rates have increased dramatically in many developed countries as a result of runaway inflation in these areas.

In order to avoid unnecessary volatility in the target life annuity payout during the decumulation (or retirement) years, and jeopardizing the objectives of self-funding and self-reliance, the level of workers' pension contributions may have to adjust in line with changes in mortality tables, the investment opportunity set, and/or government bond yields. Further, periods of pandemic disease, as experienced recently, can lead to long bouts of unemployment — and lower savings rates — which could lead to pension underfunding.

Indeed, the COVID-19 pandemic has led to many countries, including Malaysia, Australia, and India, allowing their retirement savers to dig into their pension pot, or to cut their contributions, in order to pay for their daily sustenance and needs. Cherian and Yan (2020a) argue, both analytically and from a policy standpoint, that there are alternatives. First, we demonstrate, through simulations, the calamitous effect that capital invasion during the accumulation stage has on cumulative account values. Second, we argue that it is the state's responsibility to address such immediate hardships and to cover individuals' basic needs. This can be done via cash transfers, the mitigation of job market disruptions by preserving jobs, and the maintenance of financial security via forbearance programmes and/or interest and principal payment deferrals.

The Appendix to this chapter provides a detailed excerpt of ideas proposed by Lassalvy (2011) to address the self-funding and self-reliance issue, and the avoidance of unnecessary volatility in contributions during the accumulation years to achieve the target life annuity payout value.

1.6 Monetization: Impact of Real Estate Ownership on Retirement Savings

Retirees who own equity in their home should be considering home monetization as part of the total portfolio mix available for their retirement income needs. After all, home ownership usually represents a significant portion of an individual's wealth; this is particularly true in Asian countries like Singapore, Malaysia, and China. Those who own 100 percent of the equity in their home (i.e., have paid off their mortgage in its entirety), *ceteris paribus*, have lower expenditures than those who have to rent their apartment or have still to pay off a mortgage. Given that the home could represent a significant portion of one's wealth and housing carry costs could represent a significant portion of one's monthly expenditures, it is only prudent to find ways to consider the real estate ownership situation of each person, and unlock the equity in one's home as needed, as part of the solution to the retirement savings "underfunding" problem.

A reverse mortgage is one way to unlock the equity in one's home to transform it into a stream of supplemental payments to the individual in retirement. The owner relinquishes some or all equity in his/her home to a bank in exchange for regular payments from the bank, which can be viewed as supplemental retirement income to plug any shortfalls in the basic public pension life annuity. However, there needs to be better and greater homeowner education about the concept of reverse mortgage, especially regarding its use as a retirement funding asset. There also should be better regulatory monitoring of the costs and terms of the reverse mortgage agreement. It has often been argued in the U.S. and UK that retirees are usually taken for a costly ride by the reverse mortgage banks! Note that homeowner property taxes, insurance premiums, and maintenance costs continue to remain the retiree's responsibility as long as they are living in the house.

Since public housing in Singapore consists of leasehold properties, the Singapore government offers what is known as the Lease Buyback Scheme (LBS). To put things in perspective, over 80 percent of Singapore's resident population live in public housing, with 90 percent of them owning the leasehold apartments they live in. In the LBS programme, apartment owners are able to monetize part of or all of the remaining lease in their apartment, which enables them to receive a stream of income payments in their retirement years via the CPF LIFE programme while continuing to reside in their apartment. This is one of the lowest-cost home monetization programmes I know of, which nicely transforms one's equity in a home into a (supplemental) life annuity in retirement. You can call it a worry-free home monetization scheme. Yet its take-up rate in Singapore is puzzlingly low, which is perhaps due to the mistaken belief that a leasehold property with a limited life would still make a good asset for bequest purposes!

1.7 Impact of Healthcare Cost on Pension Contributions and Distributions

Healthcare costs and medical needs tend to rise exponentially for most people during their retirement years. Given that healthcare is one of the fastest rising expenses of all retirement expenditures, there is a need to provide an efficient vehicle that provides for future outpatient, hospitalization, and major healthcare needs. There needs to be a government-mandated basic health insurance programme for all for life, which also draws on the principle of self-funding and self-reliance, one that integrates stable insurance premium payments into the lifecycle retirement contribution and distribution programme, such that it covers the retiree for all his or her basic healthcare needs, irrespective of age, preconditions, and medical bill size. It should be government mandated, so that we do not run into the "adverse selection" problem, where only the unhealthy or higher-risk individuals buy health insurance. There should also be safeguards and incentives in place to ensure that individuals do not overspend on unnecessary (and usually highly subsidized) public healthcare. Healthcare economists refer to this problem as "moral hazard".

The health insurance for life scheme can be coupled with a tax-advantaged personal Medical Savings Account, accumulated during one's working years that supplements the payment of medical bills or tops up those involving elective healthcare procedures, which do not normally fall under the life-threatening category.

Singapore has both schemes in place — they are called MediShield Life and MediSave, respectively — coupled with an excellent public healthcare system.

1.8 Conclusion

I have argued in this chapter that individuals have three fundamental concerns during retirement. These are (1) receiving a reasonable level payout every month, that (2) lasts for as long as one lives, and that (3) is indexed to one's standard of living. In other words, an average retiree would like to receive a level, inflation-indexed payout for life that enables her to maintain her standard of living. I then focused on the role of the state in the retirement savings system; more specifically, I have discussed what should be its objectives and how to achieve them.

The government should mandate a compulsory public social security savings scheme, which is self-funded for most of its members, so as to ensure that all retirees receive a basic living pension that does not severely compromise the basic standard of living. Those who fall between the cracks, i.e., the low-income population, should receive a reasonable level of social and public assistance — as well as equal opportunities — so that they can work towards self-reliance.

A goals-oriented approach to a publicly mandated retirement savings scheme will ensure retirement adequacy for all. This will address longevity and inflation risks with the provision of guaranteed life annuity and life health insurance schemes in retirement, supplemented by a home monetization programme to address any shortfalls. Any additional retirement savings and supplemental distributions in retirement would be optional and managed by the private sector, albeit in a fiduciary manner with an appropriate level of oversight by the authorities.

Appendix: Excerpted with Permission from Lassalvy (2011)

Large fluctuations in required pension contributions would create unbearable disposable income uncertainties for people with below-average revenues. As such, the public pension system should aim at achieving a double objective: self-funding and self-reliance on one side, and reasonable and stable contributions on the other. Lassalvy in 2011 described three complementary features that should help achieve this double objective:

First, at each individual's level, instead of targeting a fully funded public pension at retirement age (i.e., where past contributions have purchased the targeted life annuity of, say, 50 percent of per capita consumption), it would be better to aim at reaching a fully funded pension a few years earlier (e.g., 10 years before retirement). In this way, there would be room to absorb negative events, like an increase in real interest rates, a plunge in capital markets, and/or short periods of unemployment, without affecting the contribution levels. Any necessary adjustments for these events would thus be made by extending the contribution period over the original date planned. A continuation of an existing contribution in the distant future does not affect today's disposable income and should be almost pain free for contributors. The contribution period extension would be capped at the beginning of the life annuity payments and only at that stage might contributions have to be increased.

Second, the longevity tables and the methodology used to derive them should be transparent, public, and be computed as scientifically as possible, without trying to be conservative or generous. If assumed life expectancy is too high, citizens would receive unfairly low life annuities for every dollar they contribute. Conversely, if assumed life expectancy is too low, the public pension plan would have a funding gap which would have to be filled later on. Any increases in the expected longevity table would have two effects: Firstly, increase future contributions necessary to achieve the target life annuity pension and, secondly, create a saving shortfall for the public pension fund (as life annuity conversion factors used in the past were too generous). The first necessary adjustment, i.e., an increase in future necessary contributions, could be made by increasing the contribution period. For the second effect, the public pension fund must assume the longevity risk, given that life annuities have already been purchased. However, a fair mechanism to reduce the longevity risk faced by the public pension fund would be to cover — on an individual basis — any existing pension fund savings shortfall by using any remaining contribution period buffer available when the individual achieves a fully funded pension. The public pension fund has invested all contributions in consumption-indexed zero-coupon government bonds across all necessary maturities to minimize the asset–liability mismatch; so, assuming that the fund keeps track of what bonds were purchased with each individual's contribution, it is straightforward to calculate each individual's savings shortfall/surplus in terms of missing/excess bonds.

Finally, the long-term moving-average consumption-indexed zero-coupon government bond prices should be used to establish the level of contributions necessary through working life, to achieve the targeted consumption-indexed life annuity. Indeed, using the current annuity conversion factors, which are based on the current prices of consumption-linked zero-coupon government bonds, results in constant and potentially significant changes to the required contribution level. For example, in periods of high real interest rates, the future value of current contributions would be small and required pension contributions very high. Note that the actual conversion of cash contributions into consumption-linked life annuities is still done at current market price, using the current prices of consumption-indexed zero-coupon government bonds. The 10-year moving average prices are used only to assess the "funding situation" of each citizen's state pension, and to determine if adjustments to the contribution period or future contribution levels are necessary. Over the long term, the difference between the two calculations should not be significant, as discount rates should oscillate around their long-term moving average. Further, in practice, each year and for each individual, the difference between the previously "anticipated" annuity conversion factor and the realized conversion factor for the current year will result in the state pension being slightly over- or underfunded. As discussed above, the necessary adjustment can be made by adjusting the contribution period, unless the final contribution date is already at the cap.

The smoothing mechanisms and initial contribution period buffer described above do not guarantee that real public pension contributions will never have to be increased. Once the contribution period has been extended up to the life annuity distributions start date (because of increase in life expectancy, increase in discount factor, and/or unemployment), the only remaining adjustment factor is to increase the contribution level. However, contribution increases should occur rarely and would be distributed over the remaining working life. Note that the contribution period buffer could also be used to support the public pension fund when it is underfunded.

2

Retirement Savings — The Seven Pillars

In two articles, one written about 8 years ago and the other more recently [see Cherian (2014) and Cherian (2020, 2021)], I expound on the seven pillars of a good retirement system. The earlier piece was first carried by Singapore's leading newspaper, *The Straits Times*. While the seven pillars apply in the more generic retirement (or social security) savings scheme context, the essay was written specifically with Singapore's Central Provident Fund (CPF) in mind initially and Hong Kong's Mandatory Provident Fund (MPF) more recently.

2.1 Pillar 1: Back to Basics

As was covered in the previous chapter, a baseline retirement savings programme should focus on basic retirement and healthcare expenses. Sticking to this objective is key. In an ensuing essay, Cherian (2017) even advises, "If it ain't broke, don't fix it. Just improve it." Indeed, many Asian economies are blessed to have had a pioneering generation of leaders who had the foresight and extraordinary prescience to come up with a mandatory, fully funded social security savings system that is able to provide for basic retirement and medical expenses with financial probity and security.

It is still not too late for those nations that do not have such a programme to do something about it, given there are sufficient examples to emulate or draw from.

Firstly, some definitions. A defined contribution (DC) plan is one in which the employee, as well as the employer in many cases, makes tax-advantaged contributions to his or her individual retirement account on a monthly basis. Singapore's Central Provident Fund (CPF), Malaysia's Employees' Provident Fund (EPF), Australia's Superannuation Scheme, and to a certain extent, Hong Kong's Mandatory Provident Fund (MPF) are examples of good DC plans.

Japan's Government Pension Investment Fund (GPIF) is an example of a defined benefit (DB) pension plan. The plan sponsor in this case promises to pay the retiree a lifelong pension, which is usually a function of last-drawn salary, tenure of service, etc. That said, in America, many corporate DB plans are going broke or are grossly underfunded. In other words, they are making promises to future retirees that they will most likely not be able to keep, hence the need for reform in many of these countries' DB plans.

The trend around the world, especially in the developed economies, is for retirement savings systems to converge on a hybrid DC/DB model, i.e., with fully funded individual accounts that accumulate over one's working years, and with limited investment and withdrawal flexibility, which convert to a life annuity upon retirement. For example, the CPF savings scheme, along with CPF LIFE (the retirement life annuity scheme issued by the Singapore government), is a unique combination of the two plans.

Many U.S. corporations with problematic DB plans are now performing pension buyin and pension buyout transactions. This is when external insurance providers are remunerated with a suitable upfront premium by the corporation, so as to oblige the external provider to take on the contractual responsibility of paying the "pension" benefits to the corporation's employees in the future on its behalf.

2.2 Pillar 2: Lead Us not Into Temptation

The temptation to dig into one's retirement pot excessively for current needs, be it for housing, medical expenses, or education, can lead to severe underfunding consequences down the road, especially at the point of retirement, which is when you need the money most. Apart from plugging those "leaks," and as Cherian and Yan (2020a) point out, it is the responsibility of the state to meet any severe exigencies faced by its citizens due to no fault of their own. Apart from the disastrous effect that digging into one's retirement pot has on terminal account values (due to the opportunity cost from the lack of compounding), it is usually the state that provides financial support during times of systemic exigencies. The latter can implement cash support, jobs support, and/or loan forbearance programmes.

In the unfortunate case where members must still prematurely dig into their retirement savings due to a severe national emergency, the state could perhaps promise to match 1-for-1 — in fact, it should double match 2-for-1, say, for the bottom 40 percent of income earners — any future contributions that the employee and the employer make when the economy recovers or takes a turn for the better.

My personal view is that retirement savings meant for future retirement expenses should not be used during the working or accumulation period, whether for ongoing education, housing, or medical needs. In the U.S., for example, distinct tax-advantaged savings programmes are offered to encourage individuals to save for those different purposes, whether through 501(c)(3) educational organizations, home mortgage interest deductions, or medical savings accounts. Not commingling these (additional future) savings with the sacrosanct retirement account leads to what behavioural finance scientists refer to as **good mental accounting**. This is when individuals are forced to budget or earmark their savings into distinct (tax-deferred) sleeves, where otherwise they could be tempted into overspending, bad financial habits, or poor financial decision-making, due to the effect of commingling these.

2.3 Pillar 3: Until Death do Us Part

As argued previously, retirement life annuities are necessary and prudent financial products that enable the retiree to meet his or her basic retirement and medical expenses on an ongoing basis. The annuity should be inflation-indexed — or better still, consumption-indexed — to take into account any rising cost of living. Given that it is a life (i.e., long-term) product, the more guaranteed it is, the better. After all, it would be excruciatingly distressful to find out in 20 years time that one's insurance provider of a deferred retirement life annuity product has gone from being "AAA"-rated to a ward of the state overnight!

In asset–liability and liability-driven investing models for retirement, a long-term bond portfolio could be structured to ensure it could meet the retiree's current and future financial obligations, see Cherian and Yan (2020b). The income stream (or total returns) generated by the portfolio on the asset side would be structured as a laddered bond portfolio to meet the expense obligations on the liability side, just as an annuity would. The problem with this approach is, firstly, both nominal and real yields are at all-time lows, with the latter even turning negative across the entire term structure for many countries. Secondly, government bond maturities usually do not extend beyond 30 years — except for a select few countries — thus making the tail risks for ageing and mortality difficult to hedge. This dual bond problem makes it challenging for private pensions to manage to asset–liability or liability-driven programs when it comes to investing retirement assets.

In a compendium essay, Cherian and Yan (2021) suggest that the burgeoning convertible bond issuance market in Asia could potentially serve a different yet related dual purpose on the retirement investing front:

1. Convertibles have the advantage of downside protection with upside potential. This is because when the market is advancing, convertible bonds become equity-like, and when the market is declining, they behave like bonds (unless they default).
2. Convertibles can benefit the investor if they stick to a portfolio of highly diversified, higher-quality convertible bonds since a convertible offers income that is usually lower than the corresponding corporate bond, but higher than the dividend yield of the stock.

2.4 Pillar 4: When Default is Good

Giving too much investment choice to retirement savers in their retirement accounts during the accumulation period (i.e., working life) can lead to a condition known as "investor paralysis" — not knowing what to invest in amid too much choice. Far better to have a few well-diversified, cost-efficient asset allocation funds that members who wish to seek higher risk-adjusted returns can easily pick from. The **default** asset allocation fund(s), for those who do not wish to deal with a plethora of confusing investment options and jargon in their retirement account, is usually low cost, well diversified and fairly conservative. The higher-risk investment strategies can be made available to those who have met a certain level of financial education proficiency or those who use a licensed financial advisor upheld to the highest fiduciary standards by the pension regulators.

To their credit, Singapore's CPF Advisory Panel had in 2016 recommended to the Singapore Government, the need to study the provision of a **Lifetime Retirement Investment Scheme (LRIS)** option within the CPF. The LRIS is meant to be a prudent, cost-efficient asset allocation solution, with or without a dynamic "glidepath" component that automatically considers the various phases of the saver's lifecycle. It is also meant for those who prefer a simple-to-understand, risk-managed product to invest and grow their surplus retirement savings in, managed in a professional and institutional manner without involving the retail investor in the underlying rocket science.

As the Advisory Panel argued, such a scheme has to be as cost-efficient as possible, which by construction requires a certain minimal amount of assets under management to qualify for the (lower) institutional rates. This "seed capital" not only allows the programme to get off the ground but also takes advantage of the lower fund fees — and thus lower total expense ratios — that are available from the economies of scale in institutional fund management, see Cherian and Yan (2019a). The programme can be managed by the pension fund itself or sub-advised by a government-linked entity, the private sector, or a combination of all three as a private-public partnership.

2.5 Pillar 5: Limit Lump-sum Withdrawals

Lump-sum withdrawals at retirement are sub-optimal. Accumulated sums should instead be annuitizable at the point of retirement into a lifelong income stream, as in Singapore's CPF LIFE programme. We may think S$404,000 saved at the point of retirement is a lot of money. But even in one of the most generous (and lowest cost) of government life annuity schemes, *viz.* the CPF LIFE, a cumulated sum of S$404,000 at age 65 translates to a mere S$2,200 per month in an immediate life annuity. There is also something of a *money illusion* phenomenon here, given that the monthly level payout is in nominal terms, i.e., it does not even consider the effects of inflation!

To boot, finance theory, behavioural finance, and anecdotal evidence inform us that the natural urge in humans is to spend lump-sum payouts at retirement, especially if one is in dire need of deferred vacations, is cash-strapped, or faced with the sudden appearance of long-lost relatives, while not realizing until it is too late that there may not be enough in the kitty for one's basic retirement needs. I therefore often say that lump-sum withdrawals at the point of retirement are sub-optimal irrespective of your religion, race, nationality, and education level.

Another sub-optimal feature that arose during the recent COVID-19 pandemic was the ability for members to raid their hard-earned retirement savings accounts in order to pay for their daily expenses, reduce the pandemic-induced financial burden, and meet their other economic exigencies, which may have been a result of job loss, income reduction, and so on. India, Australia, and Malaysia famously allowed for this *ownself-help-ownself* feature, which resulted in even less money being available in members' accounts for retirement.[1]

For example, the Australian government allowed individuals to withdraw up to A$20,000 (US$15,445) from their superannuation funds by the middle of 2021. India allowed its Employees Provident Fund members to withdraw the lower of either 75 percent of their retirement savings or 3 months of their salary equivalent. And Malaysia's Employees Provident Fund (EPF) announced in March 2020 that the contribution rate for employees would be cut from 11 percent to 7 percent of their salaries and that members could withdraw a total of RM6,000 (US$1,465) over the following 12 months. Furthermore, the Malaysian government, in November 2020, announced a second withdrawal scheme of up to RM60,000 — a 10-fold increase — to "help EPF members reeling from the economic fallout of the coronavirus crisis", and a final programme that allowed members to withdraw up to a maximum of RM5,000.

---

[1] This is Singlish speak for each citizen being left to fend for himself or herself. Opinion | Do You Speak Singlish? — *The New York Times*, 13 May 2016. https://www.nytimes.com/2016/05/14/opinion/do-you-speak-singlish.html.

In total, there were three government withdrawal programmes allowed in Malaysia, i-Lestari, i-Sinar, and i-Citra, which resulted in over RM100 billion (US$24 billion) being disbursed to 7.4 million EPF members financially affected by the pandemic. According to the EPF, this was one-tenth of its AUM of RM1 trillion (US$240 billion) in national defined contribution assets and close to half of the fund's total membership at that time.

The dire situation led to the EPF's leadership sounding the alarm that — post this three-phased withdrawal programme — only 3 percent of its members could afford to retire, more than 80 percent of the EPF members who are 1 year away from their official retirement age do not have more than the recommended RM240,000 (US$57,160) in their savings accounts, over 40 percent (6 million members) have less than RM10,000 in their EPF accounts, and a staggering 30 percent (3.6 million) have less than RM1,000 socked away for retirement.[2,3]

This just isn't a good approach. There has to be a better way to address national hardship during a systemic crisis, such as the recent pandemic, instead of raiding individuals' retirement savings accounts. As I argue in Cherian and Yan (2020a), and again in Cherian (2021), early withdrawals simply destabilize the retirement plan's long-term mission of safeguarding everyone's financial future, especially in retirement. As I demonstrated in those essays, retirement account values can differ a fair bit over a long investment runway (from 1990 to 2019 in the example) due to a reduced contribution rate (10 percent instead of 11 percent) or a legislated raid on remaining principal (e.g., US$39,000 withdrawn in 1993) against the unrestricted, fully invested case. To illustrate this shortfall, I created a hypothetical 60/40 retirement portfolio that was invested in the S&P500 (60 percent) and Barclays U.S. Aggregate Bond Index (40 percent) and then subjected to each value-reducing scenario. In this particular example, the difference could be up to 18 percent over the investment horizon (see Figure 2.1).

---

[2] Only 3 percent of EPF members can afford to retire, *Asia Asset Management*, 2 November 2021. https://www.asiaasset.com/post/25222-epfretirement-gte-1101;

[3] KWSP — EPF Opens Applications For I-Citra Withdrawal. https://www.kwsp.gov.my/-/epf-opens-applications-for-i-citra-withdrawal.

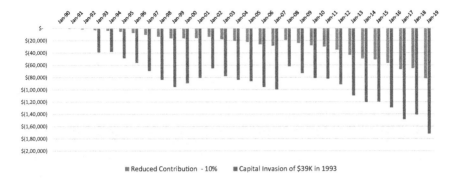

Figure 2.1: Difference in Cumulated values against full contribution of 11 percent and no capital invasion

Note: Difference in retirement account values between the unrestricted account with 11 percent contribution and no early withdrawal and (1) account with the 10 percent reduced contribution through the entire period and (2) account with early withdrawal of US$39,000 in 1993.

Source: Bloomberg; "Ring-fencing pensions," Joseph Cherian and Emma Yan, *Asia Asset Management*, May 2020, Vol. 25, No. 5.

Due to the temptation of members — sometimes with the assistance and encouragement of the government — to dig into their retirement nest eggs, my recommendation was to ringfence retirement savings accounts against such behaviour by legislation. This behaviour is understandable since retirement funds are an easy target — they tend to be the most liquid and largest pool of assets in the public's overall portfolio (apart from the accumulated equity in their homes).

Fortunately, national retirement schemes in Singapore and Hong Kong wisely resisted this temptation. Rather, Singapore simply deferred by a year a scheduled increase in the contribution rates for older workers.

So, whose responsibility is it to provide for individuals' hardship during a systemic crisis? If people face dire economic circumstances due to a national crisis, it is the state's responsibility to step in and address it. It can do so via various intervention schemes. The recent COVID-19 pandemic crisis saw many governments introducing targeted cash transfers, preserving or enhancing jobs, facilitating forbearance programmes for loan repayments, and even subsidizing the monthly contributions that members and/or employers make to members' retirement accounts.

On the positive side, pension schemes around the world are now considering life annuities, which are often inflation-indexed, as part of their retirement scheme's product offering during members' decumulation phase. This is in order to stretch their retirement dollars further into the future.

2.6 Pillar 6: Monetize Your Home if Need be

One's home, especially if it is a leasehold residence that is not expected to remain within the family for generations to come, is a perfect asset to monetize so as to supplement the homeowner's income in retirement.

To that end, Hong Kong's Mortgage Authority and Singapore's Housing Board have various low-cost home monetization programmes available for their members, which enable them to either extract the equity (in the case of Hong Kong) or sell the remaining lease left in their home (in Singapore's case). This in turn helps improve the members' financial situation in retirement. The supplemental income stream generated from a reverse mortgage or lease buyback (home monetization) scheme is invariant to the level of retirement savings cumulated. Rather, it is a function of the accumulated value of the equity (or remaining lease period left) in your home: the higher the equity value (or lease years left), the higher the income that can be extracted.

More recently, Cagamas, which is Malaysia's National Mortgage Corporation, began offering a fairly decent reverse mortgage programme that provides the following[4]:

- **lifetime tenure**: fixed monthly payouts throughout the entire life of the borrower(s),
- **no repayment during lifetime**: repayment only due when borrower(s) pass away,
- **residing in own home**: borrower(s) can stay in their home for life,
- **non-recourse**: shortfall risk upon sale-at-death is not the responsibility of the borrowers' estate.

---

[4] Malaysia's Cagamas launches 100 million ringgit reverse mortgage, country's first. *Asia Asset Management*, 24 December 2021. https://www.asiaasset.com//post/25494.

Note that all of the above national home equity monetization programmes are not only cost-efficient but also come with some form of a government-guaranteed shelter-for-life assurance, i.e., one is able to stay in one's own home until death.

2.7 Pillar 7: Continuing Education

Basic financial and retirement savings education is good and important for all. It is the responsibility of the state — and educational institutions — to provide ample public education programmes for acquiring the right level of financial knowledge, literacy, and readiness for all. We are, after all, talking about protecting and growing our life retirement savings.

Citizens also need to be, and should be, educated about, and aware of, our rights, the laws, and the regulations governing our retirement savings. This way, there is hope of recourse when something goes awry. In America, for example, the Employee Retirement Income Security Act of 1974 (ERISA) sets the "minimum standards for most voluntarily established retirement and health plans in private industry to provide protection for individuals in these plans." Failure to comply with this federal law can lead to litigation, and in some cases, criminal prosecution.

However, financial education or the threat of criminal prosecution is not the panacea for our retirement savings and planning woes. Indeed, some fundamental decision-making with respect to national retirement savings must be administered benevolently and transparently at the state level, i.e., it should not be left entirely to the fee-gouging, product-pushing private sector, as is sadly the case in Hong Kong.

2.8 Conclusion

In this section, I have laid out the seven pillars that can guide the development of a sound retirement savings programme. Some amount of decision-making with respect to the national retirement savings scheme must be mandated and laid out clearly at the state level. It is simply a fairer and more cost-efficient way to conduct retirement business for all citizens. It also enables efficient risk-sharing in the aggregate when all citizens participate in such programmes, be it for retirement savings, life annuity schemes, or health insurance for life.

3

Making a Good Programme Even Better*

3.1 Introduction

Nobel Prize-winning economist Robert Merton has said that a goal-oriented approach to retirement savings would likely yield an inflation-protected income at retirement, but would not result in wealth accumulation. Indeed, this way of thinking has perhaps resulted in the savings and life annuity payout components of our current CPF system. This is good news.

We take it that people planning for retirement have three main concerns about retirement funding: First, that they receive a reasonable payout every month; second, that the payouts should last for as long as they live; and third, that the payouts keep pace with inflation. The CPF Minimum Sum, which is converted into a CPF Life annuity product upon an individual's retirement, broadly meets these concerns. However, the CPF Life annuity payout is not inflation indexed.

Should the concerns over retirement funding end there? Not really. Individuals should also consider if retirement funding can give them the standard of living they want or are used to. We think that qualified members of the CPF — and by this, we mean those who have the potential to accumulate (or have accumulated) more than the mandatory Minimum Sum during their productive working years — should be allowed to

---

* This chapter is excerpted from NUS Lee Kuan Yew School of Public Policy's IPS Commons (2014). See Cherian and Yong (2014).

participate in an enhanced retirement savings scheme, where they can benefit from the long-term performance of well-diversified portfolios.

For convenience, let's call this enhanced scheme CPF "SoShiok" Life. It has two features not found in today's CPF scheme. First, the standard life annuity monthly payout component (say, the estimated S$1,200 per month generated from a Minimum Sum of S$155,000) will be inflation indexed annually. Second, members will be allowed to invest any savings in excess of the Minimum Sum in a number of well-diversified portfolios, depending on their risk tolerance level.

3.2 The Mechanics of CPF "SoShiok" Life

How would such a retirement savings product work? It would require some tweaks to the existing CPF system. First, unlike in the current system, CPF savings would be directed purely to retirement expenses and not used for other means, such as housing down payments and deposits, children's education, and current medical expenses. Second, a mandatory portion of CPF savings would be "ring fenced" in a Minimum Sum Retirement Account (MSRA), which would cumulate at the CPF's current, tax-exempt riskless interest rate range of 2.5 to 5 percent (preferably, this rate should be inflation indexed) up until retirement. Upon retirement, the inflation-indexed CPF Life annuity — with income deemed sufficient to cover basic life needs and medical insurance payments from retirement to death — is purchased using funds from the MSRA account.

By "ring-fencing" a portion of CPF savings, those who have managed to save more than the requisite Minimum Sum will have the opportunity to enhance their retirement nest egg. An optional "SoShiok" Retirement Account (SSRA) can be set up in parallel to the MSRA. Any CPF savings over and above that which is mandated towards the MSRA can cumulate in this SSRA account at the default riskless interest rate, say, the current 2.5–3.5 percent interest on Ordinary Accounts (OA), or a range of long-term performance of well-diversified portfolios with different investor risk tolerance levels, such as conservative, moderate, or aggressive, chosen by the CPF member. At retirement, the cumulated savings in the SSRA can be used to purchase a CPF "SoShiok" Life annuity product, which pays according to the long-term performance of another (or the

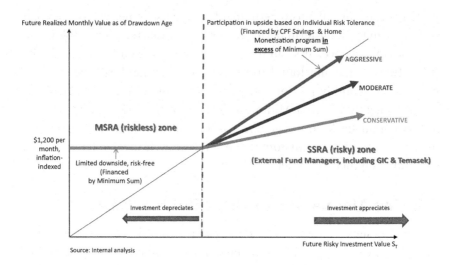

Figure 3.1: The CPF "SoShiok" life product: Inflation-indexed floor with upside potential

same) well-diversified portfolio with a particular investor risk tolerance level. As Figure 3.1 indicates, if the performance of this portfolio for a particular year is below zero, the retiree will only receive the default monthly payout from the standard CPF Life annuity and nothing from the CPF "SoShiok" Life annuity. And in the good years, if the payout is above zero, the retiree receives income from both, the Life Annuity and the SoShiok Annuity.

Needless to say, the administration of the joint MSRA and SSRA programmes during the savings years should be user-friendly, seamless, and fully transparent to members once they have made their voluntary investment choices. This same philosophy should apply to the retirement income payout years as well.

Such an "incremental" product has no element of regret: If the well-diversified portfolio loses money in a particular year, as most risky portfolios did during the Global Financial Crisis of 2008–09, there will be no gnashing of teeth or beating of breasts since retirees would still receive the basic CPF Life riskless annuity payout. And in a good year (or years), the retiree gets to participate in the upside performance of the CPF "SoShiok" Life annuity product by receiving additional income in that retirement year.

3.3 Making the Enhancement Work

Most defined contribution plans give contributors free rein to make investment decisions. But some people develop investor paralysis when faced with too many investment options. It would be helpful to have a user-friendly and limited menu of a range of well-diversified, low-cost portfolios that suit different investor risk tolerance levels. A portfolio for conservative investors could, for example, comprise stakes of roughly 80 percent of its assets in high-quality bonds and cash, with the remaining 20 percent in high-quality, blue chip stocks. The portfolio for moderate investors could comprise roughly 50 percent in bonds, cash, and convertibles, with the remaining 50 percent in stocks, commodities, and lower-volatility hedge funds. For aggressive investors, their portfolio could comprise 30 percent in bonds and convertibles, with the remaining 70 percent in stocks, commodities, and higher-volatility hedge funds. Given the popular demand for GIC's and Temasek's returns, the longer-term total returns of such government-linked portfolios could also be thrown into the pot. They are after all well-diversified portfolios themselves.

3.4 Conclusion

Our suggestions are aimed at making the CPF scheme even better. Yet, we recognize that ensuring optimum retirement savings for Singaporeans also depends on a variety of other factors. Here are some additional caveats, comments, and suggestions on how to improve our social security savings scheme.

They include the following:

1. We should not encourage CPF members to dig into their retirement pot (which is meant for life expenses and healthcare needs in retirement) to finance kids' education and that dream HDB home along the way. Education and housing programmes should be run as separate tax-advantaged programmes, like in the U.S.
2. The HDB's home monetization schemes can supplement one's retirement income by a lot, for example, the HDB 30-year Lease-Buyback Monetization Scheme; however, such schemes should guarantee participants housing for life.

3. Singapore also has the privately managed Supplementary Retirement Scheme (SRS), where citizens and Singapore Permanent Residents can contribute up to an additional S$12,750 per annum with full tax breaks to their retirement scheme. Young working adults should be encouraged to participate in this programme.

4. The CPF should also allow spouses, for example, full-time housewives or stay-at-home husbands, to participate in the CPF savings and payout scheme on equal terms as the working population, i.e., give the families who'd like to save more for their retirement the ability to do so.

4

A Word on (Retirement Savings) Costs and Longevity

High fees, like early withdrawals and cutting into your retirement principal, can erode investment returns and cumulated values. When citing high fees, I do not just recommend low-cost funds, rather the most cost-efficient ones commensurate with the skill, risk-adjusted performance, and track record of the manager.

4.1 Fees can Fleece

In an interview with *The Business Standard* in 2012, and in Cherian (2018), I challenged Asian retirement funds to follow the lead of the institutional retirement plans in the U.S., UK, and the Netherlands, where the "all-in" fees for both private and public sector plans are kept to a minimum, sometimes even regulated accordingly. Their financial advisers, additionally, are held to a high fiduciary standard. Hong Kong, Singapore, Malaysia, and Taiwan have some of the highest front-end sales loads (or subscription commissions), which sometimes run up to 5 percent upfront, and annual management fees, which can be as high as 2 percent per annum. Additionally, distributors may receive "retrocessions", an annual trailing commission paid out of the management fees of the mutual fund or Investment-Linked Insurance Policy (ILP) by the asset manager or insurance company, respectively. All these add up to what is known as the Total Expense Ratio of the product. What is even more disconcerting is that some of the aforementioned fee-gouging activity is not disclosed transparently to investors.

The good news is that the retirement plans in the above Asian countries are taking — or have already taken — major strides to either eliminate sales loads entirely or reduce them drastically, while management fees have been nudged down for those "permissioned" to be offered on the retirement system platform for members' investment purposes. For example, both the EPF in Malaysia (at least for its **EPF i-Invest** online investment scheme) and Singapore's **CPFIS** scheme have removed all sales charges for funds sold within their retirement investment scheme. Management fees have also been coming down of late.

Everyone, from regulators, investors, and advisors to asset managers, would agree that high fund and sales-related expenses significantly erode investment returns. That is exactly why U.S. Federal laws, via the ERISA, require those managing private sector retirement plans to be held to a much higher fiduciary standard than, say, financial brokers and that advice and services provided to such private retirement schemes, like 401(k) plans, are necessary and the costs reasonable. Similarly, the UK and the Netherlands have banned sales commissions and shifted the focus of financial intermediaries towards client-centric advice as opposed to commissions. Many of these same authorities have also introduced mechanisms and penalties to prevent the "churning" of retirement funds, which also erodes investment returns. Many of the aforementioned countries and retirement plans have already instituted such "churning" safeguards.

Fees can dramatically reduce one's retirement savings. That is why fee transparency is key, so that members are aware how much in fees they are paying. For example, a 5 percent sales charge on a $10,000 investment in a mutual fund nets the financial advisor $500 right off the bat, simply for the "advice" or "selling" services he provides. As a consequence, only $9,500 gets invested. Additionally, as Cherian (2018) points out, for someone who invests $1,000 a year, and receives investment returns of about 6 percent per annum on average, a 1 percent annual management fee will reduce his investment by close to 20 percent at the end of 30 years. This is as compared to, for the sake of argument, a zero-fee investment, i.e., $83,802 versus $68,881. This implies that close to one-fifth of his investment returns will be foregone due to fees, without even considering the impact inflation has on reducing purchasing power!

The moral of the story: Keep sales charges and brokerage commissions very low, preferably 0 percent, and annual management fees for the fund as cost efficient as possible, i.e., by utilizing the help of a responsible and fiduciary-minded financial advisor, picking funds that are commensurate with the skill, risk-adjusted (net of fee) performance, and track record of the asset manager.

4.2 Longevity Hurts

In Cherian and Yan (2019b), we argue that many pension plans around the world are making promises that they cannot keep given the structure of Defined Benefit (DB) plans. They promise employees an annuity for life upon retirement, which is usually a function of their years of service, age, and last-drawn salary. This long-term, outsized set of financial obligations on the part of the firm's pension fund has resulted in many DB plans, both private and public, either freezing, eliminating, converting, or outsourcing their plans. In the case of outsourcing, U.S. firms like Lockheed Martin and Boise Cascade have started handing their DB plans over to external insurance providers through pension buy-in or buyout transactions. This was an expensive proposition until recently as interest rates were low for the past decade. Other private sector DB plans, including IBM and a few legacy airlines, as well as public sector ones, especially a few California municipalities, have had to either freeze or eliminate their DB plans entirely.

The biggest worry that countries with declining population demographics have is that their retirees outlive their retirement savings. Indeed, the World Economic Forum's June 2019 report, which studied the link between life expectancy and retirement savings across six major developed nations, discovered that people would outlive their retirement savings by between 8 and 20 years on average, with the shortfall burden felt most acutely by women (Figure 4.1).

Taiwan, Malaysia, Japan, and China are some of the Asia-Pacific countries that have unsustainable pension schemes, due to their fixed age of retirement, declining fertility, and increasing longevity. Taiwan has

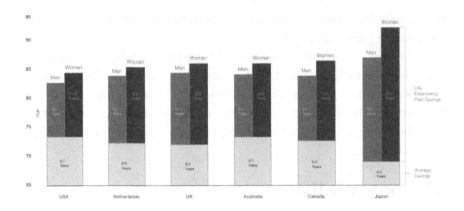

Source: World Economic Forum Analysis

Figure 4.1:   Retirement savings deficit — Years saved vs life expectancy

already started the process of reforming their scheme. The employee and the government now have to co-contribute towards future pension benefits. Adjustments have also been made to contribution and distribution rates, extending the retirement age, and attenuating the overall benefits received. China continues to aggressively explore ways to reform their pension and retirement savings system. Indeed, China's 2019 Pension Fund Actuarial Report, by the Centre for International Social Security Studies (CISSS) in the Chinese Academy of Social Sciences, indicates that pension fund monies will run out by 2035 if there is no government action taken to ameliorate the severe pension underfunding problem. Malaysian government pensioners' retirement benefits are such that they are not only adjusted annually for the cost of living (COLA) but are also extended to a deceased pensioner's dependents when he or she passes away!

Cherian and Yan (2019b) discuss three ways in which to rein in Asia's expansionary pension obligation problem:

1. Slowly and steadily convert the defined benefit plans to defined contribution plans.
2. Extend the retirement age for those who are able and willing to work.

3. Encourage more retirement savings at any point in one's working career through tax incentives (be they via tax deferrals or tax exemptions), matching contributions, and one-off "windfall" grants and top-ups.

It is also important to allow for supplementary tax-deferred or tax-free private-sector-managed retirement programmes, so that those who wish to save more for retirement can easily do so.

4.3 Conclusion

Making promises one cannot keep is not a good thing. It is high time to convert DB plans to DC plans that are self-funded — but not entirely self-directed — and yet government guaranteed in some form or other. Government policy should also be designed such that the appropriate top-down behavioural nudges, financial subsidies, and financial literacy programmes can be provided to encourage people to save more for tomorrow.

5

A Vignette on the State of the Asset Management Industry

A thriving retirement industry is a testament to the quality of the asset management industry servicing it. In an earlier chapter, I argued that high fund management fees can erode investment returns and retirement savings values. While I do not propose that all funds be low cost, I advocate most cost-efficient ones that are commensurate with the skill, risk-adjusted performance, and track record of the manager.

5.1 Asset Management Industry: Tipping Points and Trends

In my 2015 article written for Asia Asset Management — and later that year with my co-author Ranjan Chakravarty for its Special 20th Anniversary Issue, see Cherian (2015a) and Chakravarty and Cherian (2015) — I argue that the asset management industry has grown exponentially in size, with PwC predicting that APAC assets under management (AUM) will outpace any other region globally in growth with a total of US$29.6 trillion in AUM by 2025, almost double the US$15.1 trillion in 2017.[1] Willis Towers Watson records that AUM at the world's 500 largest asset managers totalled US$104.4 trillion in 2019, which is thrice the AUM of US$35.2 trillion in

---

[1] "Asset & Wealth Management 2025: The Asian Awakening (Asia Pacific)," PwC Research & Insights, January 2019. URL: https://www.pwc.com/sg/en/asset-management/assets/asset-management-2025-asia-pacific.pdf.

2000.[2] The top 20 Asian asset managers, particularly those in Japan, China, and Singapore, cumulated US$7.2 trillion in AUM in 2019, a 57 percent increase year over year.

Change and disruption are inevitable in such a large and growing industry. It falls upon the industry itself to comprehend and keep up with these changes and trends, or be left behind.

I have discussed how the asset management industry has moved to a core–satellite paradigm, where lower-cost, beta-driven strategies form the core, and highly specialized alpha-generating investment strategies serve as satellites. I summarize below the conclusions regarding drivers of this paradigm shift.

5.2 Size

According to the Willis Towers Watson Thinking Ahead Institute's 2020 report, the world's top 20 asset managers by AUM managed close to 43 percent of the US$104.4 trillion in total AUM, with BlackRock accounting for a whopping US$7.43 trillion, Vanguard around US$6.12 trillion, and Boston's SSgA and Fidelity managing US$3.12 trillion and US$3.04 trillion, respectively. Much of these assets are managed according to the core approach, be it in passive, ETF, or enhanced index strategies. So, the core part of the core–satellite approach is firmly entrenched, and the expectation is that this trend will continue to dominate and grow in both size and concentration. It will certainly account for the largest chunk of total assets under management, just as the core–satellite paradigm predicts.

This brings us to the more interesting satellite portion of the core-satellite model. This area is made up of active managers, hedge funds, private equity, and venture capital, and other so-called alpha strategy manufacturers of specialized, higher-fee investment strategies, particularly in the alternative investments space.

Simple calculus will yield that the opposite will hold true in the satellites, given the fact that competition is not only increasing among these alpha managers but that the global AUM share is fast shrinking

---

[2] "The world's largest asset managers — 2020," Thinking Ahead Institute, Willis Towers Watson, October 2020. URL: https://www.thinkingaheadinstitute.org/research-papers/the-worlds-largest-asset-managers-2020/.

in this segment. Nevertheless, according to the Monetary Authority of Singapore's "2019 Singapore Asset Management Survey," the alternatives sector in Singapore registered year-over-year growth of 12 percent as of end December 2019, reaching a peak of S$721 billion (US$536.2 billion), mostly led by private equity and venture capital managers. The AUM from both these asset classes occupied 35.2 percent of the total AUM allocated to alternative investments in Singapore, with its AUM across all asset classes growing by 15.7 percent year over year to hit S$4.0 trillion (US$2.9 trillion) by end December 2019. Yet my research — see Cherian, Kon, and Weng (2016) — registered almost 1 in 2 Asian hedge funds ceasing to operate between 2000 and 2012!

Nevertheless, the scale players will dominate the core space, where I expect even greater consolidation and M&A, the lowering of fees, and systematic strategies — such as exchange traded funds (ETFs) and passive investing strategies — to dominate simply from the available economies of scale.

On the other hand, the satellite programmes will see further fragmentation, as the industry transforms and is disrupted. As AI and robots move into the alpha space, purely human-led investment strategies will have their work cut out for them; there will be diminishing returns to the more expensive proprietary research, which will play a key role in determining if the manager has an investment edge.

As the satellite providers ("alpha generators") shrink in both AUM and numbers, perhaps only the truly good alpha players will remain in play. For example, we can imagine a world where only hedge funds like Citadel, Millenium, and Renaissance survive in the non-core space. Although these managers are huge by hedge fund standards, their assets under management pale in comparison to the core managers like BlackRock and Vanguard.

That said, I predict that strengths such as long-term, time-consistent, and good risk-adjusted performance, low portfolio manager turnover, and value-added differentiators will see these satellite managers through this monopolistic competition phase for alpha, as larger alpha producers gobble up smaller ones. This does not preclude the behemoth core players from gobbling up the smaller alpha ones, or the reverse, viz., the larger satellites acquiring the smaller players in the core! Long-term institutional backing, perhaps from well-regarded sovereign and private equity funds, could help expedite this process.

As in the asset-backed securities market of old, the infrastructure asset manager's domain expertise — at the issuer, counterparty credit appraisal and risk hedging, guarantee, and development levels — would deliver tremendous value add. Thanks to the straight-through financial ecosystem model approach, the infrastructure asset manager will be able to greenfield, brownfield, structure and finance, develop, and manage infrastructure, all under one umbrella holding company. They will hence be well compensated in this area over the next 5 to 10 years.

5.3 Skill

I have already mentioned that long-term, time-consistent, and good risk-adjusted performance is central to survival in the satellite (or alpha-producing) investments space. However, instead of regurgitating well-known facts about alpha generation, whether from fundamental research or quantitative multifactor research, I would like to highlight asset classes where there are opportunities for managers to add tremendous value.

We are already seeing such entities forming and operating with the help of multilateral banks and/or government-linked funds. One such firm that comes to mind is Surbana Jurong (SJ). SJ is a Temasek-owned global urban, infrastructure, and managed services consulting firm. In addition, SJ has nine member companies that bring various specialized skillsets to the table. These are in addition to Surbana Jurong Capital, the financial investment arm that "sources, plans, invests, develops, and manages projects across the entire value chain of the urbanization, industrialization, and infrastructure domains." I discuss in greater detail this innovative infrastructure financing model undertaken by Surbana Jurong Capital in the following section, where sustainability, cost efficiency, and integrating the asset/liability management of all parties involved to improve everyone's lifecycle balance sheet management, while funding critical infrastructure projects, are core to the firm's mandate and operations.

Another area of innovation is in the retirement finance space. Numerous goals-based retirement solutions and financial products now exist in the U.S., Europe, and even Asia. Lifecycle funds with glidepath trajectories are becoming popular. Yet, these constitute a second-best solution in our quest to attain adequate retirement income, where the cumulating retirement savings portfolio de-risks with the passage of time up until the point of retirement. They are second best because the one-size-fits-all glidepath approach for groups or cohorts of savers is not particularly customized to the individual's special needs, retirement goals, risk aversion, human capital situation, etc.

Furthermore, the lifecycle approach does not guarantee a smooth transition from the accumulation phase to the decumulation phase, where an adequate income stream is needed in retirement to maintain one's standard of living for life (pre- and post-retirement). The CPF Scheme in Singapore is an example where the transition is indeed fairly smooth; retirement sufficiency, adequacy, or inflation indexing aside, cumulated savings in the CPF Scheme at the point of retirement can be automatically converted to a government-administered life annuity programme called CPF LIFE.

There are two attendant retirement design issues that have not been addressed: (1) provision of inflation-protected retirement income for life and (2) creation of "pension bonds" (a.k.a. deferred life annuities), in the absence of a Defined Benefit programme, which investors can easily and efficiently purchase during their accumulation phase so as to automatically meet their retirement income needs.

Various inflation protection products already exist in the marketplace, but investing in them requires some level of sophistication. Furthermore, as opposed to buying and holding a *U.S. Treasury Inflation-Protected Security (TIPS)* directly, with a guaranteed amount of inflation-protected cash over a particular maturity, an inflation-protected mutual fund is usually managed as a total return product, with no specific maturity date at worst or a certain duration at best. As a result, the "real" payoff at a future date to the investor is uncertain.

To meet the need for both inflation protection and lifetime income in retirement, Nobel laureate Robert Merton proposes an innovative inflation-indexed, deferred life annuity government "pension bond" product called *Standard-of-Living, Forward-starting, Income-only Securities (SeLFIES)*. SeLFIES help achieve the individual's retirement savings and goals with respect to adequacy, security, longevity, and cost-of-living adjustments, without the individual having to be hugely literate, sophisticated, or savvy in the financial or investment sense.[3]

When it comes to skill, the key differentiator will be its replicability by the satellite asset managers. If replicable, the "alpha" (or satellite product) could be acquired by a core firm and scaled, hence leading to the lowering of costs, until the marginal costs outweigh the marginal benefits, at which point, it, too, becomes a core product!

5.4 Process

Process is the capability of having a systematic approach (or discipline) in the conduct of the asset management business. It could be the way in which models, alpha, or value is systematically added to the investment process, or in the risk measurement, management, and reporting function. Strides made in Big Data and the associated analytics help facilitate this process.

After financial market-moving experiences such as the Global Financial Crisis and COVID-19 pandemic, investors have become even more concerned about risks arising from excess market volatility, draw downs, and tail risks. As a consequence, transparency and simplicity in risk reporting are necessary.

On the analytical side, much has been learned from the numerous "black swan" events in the financial services industry over the last 30 years, including the study of expected risks and drawdowns using Monte Carlo simulations, Value at Risk (VaR), and backtesting. Regulatory frameworks, rules, and lessons from the banking and insurance industry, which include Basel II/III and Solvency II, hedge efficiency testing, and stress testing, are also helpful to the asset management industry if appropriately transported and implemented.

In summary, risk management in a Big Data world has to be as state of the art — and commensurate in importance — as the alpha-generating models and processes.

---

[3] Merton, Robert C. and Muralidhar, Arun, "SeLFIES: A new pension bond and currency for retirement" (March 4, 2020). URL: https://ssrn.com/abstract=3548319.

5.5 Conclusion

The asset management industry is experiencing more regulation, risk aversion, volatility, and malaise. And with technological disruption and transformation close on the heels of our industry, one can argue that ours may end up a sunset industry. Indeed, ETFs/ETNs, Nutmeg, Yu'e Bao, robo-advisors such as Syfe and Endowus, and other FinTech developments (with the help of AI) are rapidly taking over the business of managing assets smartly.

Yet, before we pen our own obituary, a deep-dive review of our business reveals that from a functional standpoint, the asset management industry will not change as dramatically as financial jargon or the start-ups proclaim. Instead, a systematic and functional approach to managing money, manufacturing financial innovations, and mitigating risks will help asset managers to continue to add value and to reap the available benefits for a long time to come.

Making Promises We Can't Keep: The Asian Pensions Predicament*

6.1 Introduction

When individuals overextend themselves by borrowing beyond their means and don't have enough assets or income to meet their debt obligations, they usually file for personal bankruptcy. It's the same with companies.

Could this happen to defined-benefit (DB) pension plans? Well, it already has in the US. Various US public and private pension plans had to either freeze, eliminate, or convert their DB plans. These plans had corporations or governments promising employees a set of life annuity payments upon retirement, which is usually a function of an employee's years of service, age, and last-drawn salary. Private sector examples include IBM and a few legacy airlines, while public sector failures include many California municipalities.

6.2 We are Not Alone — The Case of Malaysia

The Malaysian government, during former Prime Minister Dr. Mahathir Mohamad's visit to Japan, announced that it will continue the pension scheme for civil servants until a new mechanism is devised to alleviate the fiscal burden, which now stands at 28 billion Malaysian ringgit (US$7

---

* This chapter is excerpted from Asia Asset Management. See Cherian and Yan (2019b).

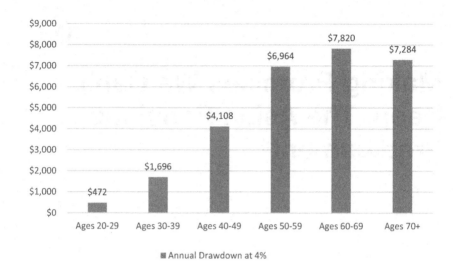

Figure 6.1:   Annual payout at 4 percent based on average 401(k) balances by age group as of Q1 2019 (USA)
Source: Fidelity Investments.

billion) annually. That's around one-third of Malaysia's 2019 budget. It has become a huge financial drain on the national coffers.

But Malaysia isn't alone in its pension predicament. It merely highlights the imminent retirement savings sustainability issues faced by both developing and developed nations, namely, the precarious funding status of their private and public pensions, and the difficulty in implementing reforms to solve the issue.

In the US, if a private sector pension plan fails to deliver on its promises, a government agency called the Pension Benefit Guaranty Corporation (PBGC) steps in to make some, but not all, the promised pension payments to retirees. Unfortunately, the PBGC has had so many private DB plan failures on its hands over the years that it is itself now grossly underfunded.

It's been estimated that the PBGC's liabilities exceeded its assets by as much as $51 billion at the end of 2018 (Figure 6.1).

6.3 When It Rains, It Pours

General Electric recently announced that the company is freezing its pension plan for approximately 20,000 salaried employees and supplementary pension benefits for approximately 700 employees who became executives before 2011 in the US. The changes will become effective in January 2021. The company had already closed its pension plan to new entrants in 2012.

In China, a comprehensive Pension Fund Actuarial Report released this year by the Centre for International Social Security Studies (CISSS) indicated that the accumulated surplus of the pension fund could possibly be used up by 2035, absent any government action.

Meanwhile, Japan's public pension liabilities amount to around 165 percent of the country's gross domestic product!

6.4 Drivers of Pension Liabilities

Factors that contribute to a pension plan's ballooning deficit include demographics, increased life expectancy, and inflation, among other things. In the case of public pensions, where benefits are funded by taxes and other state-provisioned income, the so-called support ratio, or the share of workers to retirees, is an important determinant as well. As birth rates drop and retirees live longer, the support ratio declines and underfunding is bound to happen.

This is also true in Asia. In most Asian developing countries, including Malaysia and China, the retirement age is fixed, birth rates are falling, and retirees are living longer.

In Malaysia, the retirement benefits of government pensioners are growing dramatically. That's because the benefits are not only adjusted annually for cost of living but they are also extended to the dependents of a civil servant who passes away while still working in government or after retiring.

In China, the CISSS report indicates that the payer-to-retiree ratio will decline from 2:1 in 2019 to 1:1 in 2020.

Taiwan, meanwhile, had to prudently reform its public pension system in order to prevent pension funds from going bankrupt. The pension system has moved from an unsustainable scheme that was completely financed by the government to one where employees and the government jointly contribute their fair share towards future benefits. Changes were also made to the savings and payout rates, retirement age, and overall benefits.

6.5 The Solution

How do Asian countries with ballooning pension liabilities address the issue? First, they should take a leaf from the US experience, and redesign and optimize risk sharing by converting DB plans into defined contribution plans, like Malaysia's Employees Provident Fund and Singapore's Central Provident Fund (CPF). Both have prudent contribution programmes, asset–liability management or liability-driven investing schemes, and in the case of the CPF, a government-administered life annuity income payout programme upon retirement.

Second, extend the retirement age so that people not only live longer but also work longer. Third, establish policies and incentives which encourage people to start saving earlier and save more. These policies should also discourage people from raiding their retirement plans for education, housing, leisure, and other interim needs during their working-age savings or accumulation period.

Fourth, since many government-administered retirement plans provide massive subsidies and transfers that can be costly, policymakers should allow for supplementary tax-deferred, or better yet tax-free, retirement programmes managed by the private sector so that those who wish to save more for retirement can do so.

There should also be a government-mandated mechanism where only prudent, well-diversified investment products — such as lifecycle funds — with low institutional-level fee structures, easy online on-boarding schemes devoid of sales charges and commissions, and independent, for-fee advice schemes acting on a fiduciary basis are allowed on such platforms.

It certainly won't be easy to transform or reform traditional pension plans overnight. The first step is for people to realize that current DB schemes in Asia lack adequacy, sustainability, and perhaps even integrity. This should go hand in hand with appropriate top-down behavioural nudges, temporary financial subsidies, and simple financial education.

6.6 Conclusion

Ultimately, the answer lies less in underlying demographic realities such as longer life expectancies and lower mortality rates, and more in the adoption of proactive policies and systems, as well as vigilant cooperation among all stakeholders, be they federal and state, or employers and employees. Hopefully, we can all eventually get there.

7

Terms of Endurement: Retirement Solutions Should Harness Investment Science and Technology to Shockproof Plans*

7.1 Introduction

Humankind has made huge strides in technology. Big data and data analytics, artificial intelligence, machine learning, and deep learning are being used in various daily applications and industries. But when it comes to retirement schemes, we appear to be stuck in the past.

The leading solution that private retirement planners have come up with is a spectrum of well-diversified risk/return investment portfolios drawn from 1950s financial technology, or at best a series of target date funds, where risk taking follows a predefined "glidepath". A recent innovation has been the enabling of the same solutions at lower cost using technology, or robo-advisers. Surely we can do better.

Asia is unique in that many countries in this region have mandatory national retirement schemes. Herein lies the benefit. A wide cross section of society participating in a national scheme not only brings the power of large-scale asset accumulation as a *tour de force* when negotiating in the

* This chapter is excerpted from Asia Asset Management (2020). See Cherian and Ong (2020).

public interest but it also provides the ability to risk pool across retirement cohorts. But herein also lies the problem. The financial industry's definition of cohorts is narrow, usually using risk tolerance, age, or time to retirement as parameters.

7.2 The Basics

Let's visit the basics. There are two phases during one's lifecycle: the accumulation phase, which is before retirement, and the decumulation phase, which is in retirement.

The priority in the accumulation phase should be on accumulating savings so as to target the income needed in retirement, with a focus on growth in future annuity value. When approaching retirement and post-retirement, the lifecycle risks are about mitigating uncertainty around the affordable, in-retirement income so that the accumulated savings can support the rest of the retiree's life.

Consequently, the retirement fund's target income investment strategy during the accumulation phase should be consistent with the way a variable deferred life annuity product is managed. It would be a bespoke function of one's age, correlation of future wage income to the returns of all assets in place, personal profile, habits, risk, and loss tolerance, among other things.

One's target income in retirement or during the decumulation phase determines the type of life annuity product generated. Mitigating uncertainty around future income generation is therefore an important consideration.

It should be obvious that both phases of the lifecycle are simply joint saving, investing and planning decisions linked by the same target life annuity product — quite unlike the way financial planners think or provide solutions for retirement currently.

These ideas are not new. Nobel laureate Robert C. Merton wrote the theory behind lifecycle finance in the 1980s and articulated it for finance practitioners in his article, "Thoughts on the Future: Theory and Practice in Investment Management", which was published in the *Financial Analysts Journal* in 2003.

Traditionally, the defined-benefit (DB) plan of a corporation or government would have taken on the responsibility of providing employees a set of life annuity payments upon retirement, which is usually a function of their years of service, age, and last-drawn salary. In theory, it's a sound principle that allows retirees to maintain some semblance of pre-retirement purchasing power, even during retirement.

However, due to lack of focus, operating budgets, and investment expertise, DB plans ended up making promises they couldn't keep. Now the decision-making responsibility has shifted to the individual through defined contribution (DC) plans. This means the burden of retirement planning falls on those who are not savvy in such matters. It's like asking patients to perform brain surgery on themselves while fully awake.

7.3 Customizing Plans

The industry needs to be awakened from its fee-induced coma. Why not establish the necessary infrastructure for big data analytics, deep learning, and investment science to create a target income-focused retirement plan that is personalized, bespoke, or customized over one's lifecycle that is also low cost from its full use of technology?

As a start, those in the accumulation phase of their lifecycle should be stratified into financial economics-driven representative cohorts that transcend age and risk tolerance so that appropriate target income investment profiles can be created for each cohort while taking advantage of risk-pooling arrangements. Representative retirement cohorts could be created using the following:

o   The current and projected human capital labour income stream and its correlation with one's investment assets in place;
o   Current retirement savings and investment, other savings, target income in real dollars, spending, investing, inheritance, and risk preference of the individual with respect to social, educational, financial, healthcare, human capital, and demographic characteristics;
o   Mapping of the key determinants of target income and risk preferences with respect to one's:
  ❖   point-in-time in lifecycle savings, contributions, and investments programme;
  ❖   personal profile and circumstances like education, current income, existing stock of retirement savings, and housing;

❖ demographic factors;

❖ risk appetite or tolerance, age or time to retirement, gender, salary, marital status, and retirement income goal(s), including providing for healthcare, leisure, and travel in retirement.

A mathematical optimization method called stochastic dynamic programming can then be used to maximize monthly (future) target income at the point of retirement. Given the discussion so far, this approach is more realistic and useful, as compared to mean-variance optimization that maximizes risk-adjusted end-of-period wealth, which our industry is fond of using.

Consider the following optimal portfolio risk allocation simulation, which a well-trained financial engineer can perform using the backward induction method from dynamic programming. For convenience, we model a median Singaporean degree-holder from age 25 to 65, and assume he saves 10 percent of his gross monthly salary in his private retirement fund, on top of his nationally mandated Central Provident Fund (CPF) contribution. The simulation assumes no management or transaction fees.

The blue bands in the chart illustrate the potential deferred annuity income values in retirement, commencing at age 65, from his private retirement fund. The median outcome of an immediate annuity at age 65 corresponds to approximately S$3,300 of inflation-adjusted retirement income per month for 20 years — assuming a life expectancy of 85 years — which isn't that bad an outcome. This would be on top of his CPF LIFE annuity payout, which currently pays between S$600 and S$2,100 per month for life to Singaporeans, depending on one's CPF balance at retirement and choice of LIFE annuity payout.

The red bands illustrate the retirement portfolio's optimal risk allocation to risky and riskless assets; some may find this graph similar to the glidepath from target date funds. The risky asset is represented by a broadly diversified global equity index, i.e., MSCI World, and the riskless asset is represented by a laddered portfolio of inflation-protected government bonds, with a duration profile matching the retirement income liabilities. Note that both outcomes and risk allocations have uncertainty — or confidence interval — bands associated with them. This is due to varying market returns, and the fact that our simulation model dynamically adjusts for that variation.

Participants in retirement plans, on the other hand, should not be bothered with the complex financial engineering involved to get the above results, be it dynamic programming, Bellman equations, or backward induction; rather, they should care more about the outcomes.

If the purpose of saving and investing for retirement is to maintain an adequate standard of living in retirement as one ages, which includes meeting healthcare costs, the investment strategy should focus on achieving an inflation-protected target income stream for life.

- The risk to be managed, therefore, is the risk of not realizing this target income goal.
- As such, the volatility of portfolio values and expected returns is not a good measure of target income shortfall risk.
- The relationship between portfolio value and lifetime retirement income depends on real interest rates and mortality rates, both of which can vary through time (Figure 7.1).

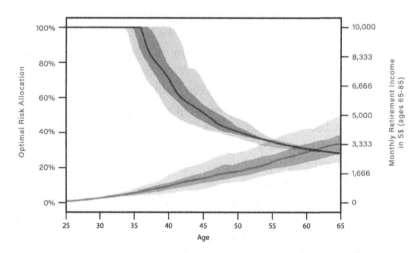

Figure 7.1:   Monthly deferred retirement income values in S$ between ages 65 and 85 (RHS, blue graph) versus optimal risk allocation between global stocks (percent shown) and inflation-protected government bonds (LHS, red graph)

Source: Bloomberg and internal dynamic programming simulations.

7.4 Conclusion

In summary, the next generation of shockproof and timeproof retirement solutions must aim to help participants achieve a unique stream of target retirement income that is sufficient to maintain their standard of living, meet in-retirement healthcare costs, protected from the ravages of inflation, and designed to last throughout their retirement years. It should also minimize the likelihood of the financial retirement industry not meeting those three fundamental objectives.

Given the complexity in the big data analytics, artificial intelligence, and financial engineering behind the design and implementation of such bespoke retirement products at the national level, it would require the best of the investment management industry, academia, and policymakers with the right mindset to come together in a public–private partnership format to structure the right solutions for our retirement. Investors deserve nothing less.

8

Algo's Got Rhythm*

Alternative investment hedge fund strategies based on algorithmic trading could become more mainstream.

8.1 Introduction

Institutional investors, who are traditionally conservative, such as pension funds, are now exploring allocating a larger portion of their assets under management to alternative or non-traditional investments. These include hedge funds, private equity, venture capital, real estate, and infrastructure.

The chart below underscores the tremendous growth in this asset class. It shows that the hedge fund industry alone had US$3.15 trillion of total assets under management as of end June 2019, more than double the figure at the end of 2011 (Figure 8.1).

8.2 The Global Trend

This is not just a US story; it's a global phenomenon. In Asia, Japan's Government Pension Investment Fund, the world's largest pension, began investing in non-traditional asset classes in 2017. The fund targets to allocate 3 percent of its $1.4 trillion of assets to alternative investments in the next 3 years.

---

*This chapter is excerpted from Asia Asset Management (2020). See Cherian and Sansi (2020).

Hedge fund industry

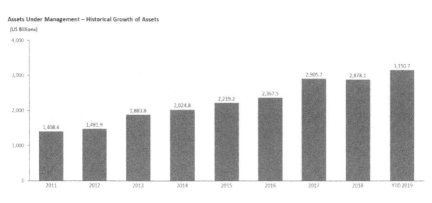

Figure 8.1: Total hedge fund assets under management (January 2011 – end June 2019)
Source: BarclayHedge, 2011–2019

Malaysia's Employees Provident Fund (EPF), which has traditionally been an investor in private equity, real estate, and infrastructure, is placing up to 10 percent into real estate and infrastructure alone. The EPF's investments in real assets include the Guoco Tower in Singapore, the Battersea Power Station development in London, and toll roads in Malaysia.

In Switzerland, according to a comprehensive annual risk study of Swiss pensions by one of its top pension consulting firms, Complementa, as quoted by IPE and top1000funds, "allocation to alternative assets has reached double digits for the first time, with investments in insurance-linked securities, private debt and infrastructure behind the growth. Around 9 percent of all pension funds currently exceed 15 percent in their allocation to alternatives."

Canada's pension funds, including the Canadian Pension Plan Investment Board and the Ontario Teachers' Pension Plan, are some of the world's most sophisticated institutional investors in alternative asset classes. Private equity and hedge funds each make up to around 20 percent of the average Canadian pension fund's portfolio.

Some may argue that the current spate of institutional allocations to alternative investments, particularly in private equity, is just "hot money" chasing the asset class. In some cases, it has even been at the expense of underperforming hedge funds. Whatever the case, alternative investments are growing rapidly.

8.3 Low Correlations to Traditional Assets

Fortunately, many finance practitioners are also believers in contrarian and behavioural strategies. In the popular factor investing space, the valuation factor (a.k.a. the Warren Buffet factor), which measures the cheapness of a security relative to its industry median, hasn't been performing well over the last few years. It is a bread-and-butter factor in many quantitative equity funds.

Yet, academic studies and empirical evidence to date indicate that the contrary is true in the long run. Perhaps this is now the time to be a contrarian and invest in beaten-up quantitative equity funds that bet on valuation.

Similarly, long/short hedge funds have been getting the rap for being underperformers of late but yet expensive. Adding to its woes, hedge fund strategies utilizing high-frequency, algorithmic, or statistical trading techniques have been accused of being black boxes, and hence lacking transparency.

However, algorithmic trading-based hedge funds created by those with combined training in financial economics, investments, and computer science do merit a closer look.

Most long-term investors, particularly asset owners like pension funds, who are looking for good hedge fund managers to invest in express a preference not only for low correlations to traditional asset classes such as equity markets but also stability in investment strategy, risk-adjusted performance, and human capital.

Figure 8.2 below indicates that the broad-based hedge fund index has had low volatility and correlation compared to the S&P 500 index. And the 36-month moving average performance chart below reinforces our observation regarding the broad-based hedge fund index having a lower volatility than the S&P 500.

Our proposition here is that an algo-driven hedge fund, which successfully marries skills in financial investments and computer science,

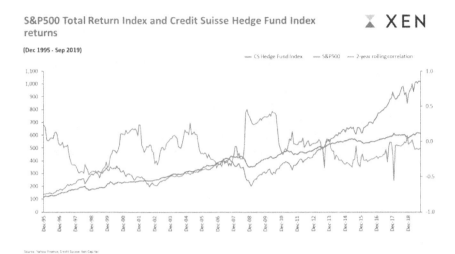

Figure 8.2:   Correlations between S&P500 Total Return Index and Credit Suisse Hedge Fund Index returns
Source: Yahoo Finance, Credit Suisse, Ken Capital

along with big data, could be the institutional investor's answer in a quest for low correlations and stability in both returns and human capital.

8.4 The "Robo CIO"

An algo fund is attractive for a number of reasons. Programme-driven strategies are systematic and disciplined. Those within scope are strategies based on sound academic research and science and which have been backtested and stress-tested over multiple market cycles to yield stable risk-adjusted returns, or alpha.

Such strategies preclude the "key man" risk issue, where the loss of a key person could affect confidence in — and hence result in the outflow of assets from — the hedge fund. All that matters for the firm's business continuity is that a team of well-trained financial economists, computer scientists, and big data analysts can translate investment research into a set of profitable hedge fund trading strategies using reams of well-commented computer programmes (Figure 8.3).

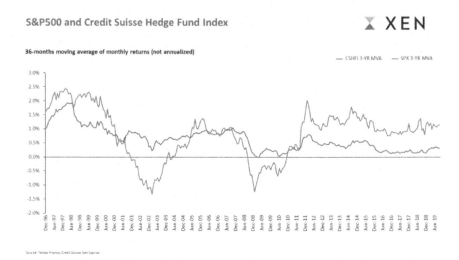

Figure 8.3:   36-months moving average of monthly S&P500 and Credit Suisse Hedge Fund
Index returns
Source: L Yahoo Finance, Credit Suisse, Xen Capital

Once this is achieved, there will also be consistent and systematic
application of the algorithmic process globally, irrespective of investment
universe, region, industry, and/or employee location.

This may sound like a scene out of a Hollywood science fiction movie,
but the chief investment officer (CIO) of such a hedge fund is also an algo.
The "robo CIO" dispassionately and scientifically selects the most optimal
risk-adjusted strategies, constructs portfolios, controls leverage, creates the
lowest-cost execution and trading strategies using state-of-the-art order
management systems, and manages portfolio risk. Human intervention is
only a last resort.

Meanwhile, humans are freed up to continually test new research ideas
and strategies, refine and update the process, ensure compliance with the
regulatory authorities, and perform client-facing activities of a humanoid
nature.

8.5 Customization is Easy

An attendant benefit of algos is that fund subscriptions and redemptions —
and, therefore, fund openings and closures — are driven by systematic,

process-driven programmes and algorithms. An algo fund, hence, will never become "too large" or take on opportunities unless the risk-adjusted alpha still exists. In other words, it will not be a consequence of capital inflows.

Finally, the customization of portfolios to an investor's desires and needs is a cinch using algos. This includes incorporating client-specific considerations concerning sustainable and responsible investing, be it environmental, social and governance, principles for responsible investments, sustainable development goals, taxes, compliance with *shariah* law in the case of Islamic bonds or *sukuk*, and so on.

8.6 Conclusion

Coming a full circle, how does all this digitalization of the investment management process benefit pension funds? For owners of long-term capital looking for hedge fund strategies that are systematic and disciplined, that can be customized for lower volatility and leverage, and automatically screened for quality, sustainability, "greening", and other criteria they care about deeply, the time of algo-driven hedge funds has probably arrived.

9

Are Hedge Funds Just Traditional Beta?*

As conservative investors turn to alternatives, let's closely analyse hedge fund strategies.

9.1 Introduction

During a comprehensive academic study with my co-authors, see Cherian, Kon, and Li (2020), as to whether Asian and US hedge fund strategies can be explained by judiciously chosen systematic linear and nonlinear risk factors, we stumbled on something interesting. Certain hedge fund strategies are truly market-neutral, while others aren't. The following commentary constitutes a preview of various hedge fund strategies' exposure to such factors.

Why is this study important? Institutional investors who traditionally are conservative, such as pension funds, are now exploring allocating a larger portion of their assets under management to alternative investments, including hedge funds, private equity, venture capital, real estate, and infrastructure. *Top1000funds* reported that Australia's US$113 billion sovereign wealth fund, the Future Fund, recently announced that it will be allocating even more money to its US$15.3 billion hedge fund programme.

According to *BarclayHedge*, as of 3rd Quarter 2022, global assets under management in the hedge fund industry had grown to US$5.03 trillion, with US$151 billion in Asian funds.

---

* This chapter is excerpted from Asia Asset Management (2020). See Cherian *et al.* (2020).

With all this money pouring into hedge funds, and given that they are not cheap — management fees still run into the 2 percent range and performance fees are at 20 percent — it behoves translational researchers to determine whether hedge funds are truly worth their salt. This chapter will expound on that topic.

9.2 Alternative Beta Blockers

Our factor exposure analysis of 2020 compared sample period betas and 24-month rolling betas of the various hedge fund index level strategies against systematic risk factors such as the market portfolio (S&P 500), commodity returns, credit spreads, downside risk (VIX), short-term hedges (PutWrite strategy), and the ubiquitous Fama-French factors. More specifically, I define the risk factors as follows:

- S&P 500: S&P 500 market index return in excess of the risk-free rate;
- Emerging market: MSCI Emerging Markets Index return in excess of the risk-free rate;
- Bond: Month-end to month-end change in the US Federal Reserve 10-year Treasury constant maturity yield minus the US Federal Reserve 3-month Treasury constant maturity yield;
- USDX: US Dollar Index return relative to the value of a basket of currencies comprising the US's most significant trading partners;
- Credit: Month-end to month-end change in Moody's BAA yield — US Federal Reserve 10-year Treasury constant maturity yield;
- DVIX: First difference of VIX, a risk aversion indicator;
- Commodity: S&P Goldman Sachs Commodity Index (GSCI) return;
- Size: Russell 2000 return — Russell 1000 return;
- Value: Russell 1000 Value return — Russell 1000 Growth return;
- Momentum: Kenneth French's momentum factor from his data library;
- Short put: CBOE S&P 500 PutWrite Index Return, a strategy that earns downside risk premium.

Using comprehensive monthly data obtained from *Eurekahedge* between January 2000 and December 2019, we plotted the 24-month rolling betas of hedge fund strategies against these risk factors to observe

Table 9.1: The period betas for various North American (NA) hedge fund strategies (first row) against various systematic risk factors (first column) over the sample period January 2000 to December 2019

		NA HF Index	NA Arbitrage	NA CTA/Managed Futures	NA Fixed Income	NA Long short equity	NA Macro	NA Multi Strategy	NA Relative Value	NA Distressed Debt	NA Event Driven
SPX	Period Beta ('00-'19)	0.33	0.18	-0.01	0.28	0.40	0.01	0.35	0.35	0.56	0.63
	S.D. of Rolling Beta	0.09	0.10	0.17	0.08	0.09	0.30	0.09	0.09	0.19	0.18
USD	Period Beta ('00-'19)	-0.38	-0.17	-0.18	-0.29	-0.31	-0.03	-0.30	-0.36	-0.56	-0.59
	S.D. of Rolling Beta	0.17	0.12	0.23	0.14	0.24	0.30	0.19	0.18	0.41	0.39
Commodity	Period Beta ('00-'19)	0.13	0.07	0.06	0.09	0.15	0.00	0.14	0.10	0.19	0.22
	S.D. of Rolling Beta	0.09	0.05	0.08	0.08	0.11	0.11	0.10	0.10	0.22	0.18
Momentum	Period Beta ('00-'19)	-0.07	-0.06	0.05	-0.13	-0.08	0.02	-0.09	-0.13	-0.21	-0.25
	S.D. of Rolling Beta	0.18	0.07	0.09	0.10	0.22	0.20	0.18	0.16	0.18	0.34
Value	Period Beta ('00-'19)	-0.16	-0.07	0.05	-0.18	-0.20	0.03	-0.20	-0.08	-0.19	-0.17
	S.D. of Rolling Beta	0.17	0.14	0.21	0.21	0.20	0.27	0.20	0.15	0.34	0.30
Credit	Period Beta ('00-'19)	-3.32	-2.74	0.32	-3.90	-4.48	0.81	-3.91	-3.91	-4.21	-4.83
	S.D. of Rolling Beta	2.34	1.27	2.69	2.86	3.11	3.27	2.18	2.48	3.87	4.54
Bond	Period Beta ('00-'19)	0.45	-0.37	-0.06	-0.13	0.77	-0.29	0.33	1.10	1.84	0.55
	S.D. of Rolling Beta	2.57	1.48	1.78	2.88	3.35	2.07	2.70	3.02	4.34	4.89
DVIX	Period Beta ('00-'19)	-0.38	-0.20	-0.02	-0.27	-0.33	0.01	-0.31	-0.27	-0.49	-0.55
	S.D. of Rolling Beta	0.08	0.10	0.16	0.10	0.08	0.21	0.10	0.09	0.15	0.13
Size	Period Beta ('00-'19)	0.30	0.11	0.06	0.21	0.37	-0.03	0.29	0.26	0.45	0.51
	S.D. of Rolling Beta	0.16	0.10	0.19	0.14	0.21	0.24	0.19	0.20	0.28	0.33
Emerging Market	Period Beta ('00-'19)	0.22	0.12	0.03	0.21	0.26	0.01	0.24	0.21	0.38	0.43
	S.D. of Rolling Beta	0.05	0.06	0.11	0.06	0.07	0.15	0.06	0.08	0.15	0.12
Short Put	Period Beta ('00-'19)	0.41	0.36	0.00	0.36	0.50	0.00	0.45	0.43	0.68	0.79
	S.D. of Rolling Beta	0.18	0.17	0.23	0.09	0.18	0.38	0.14	0.15	0.25	0.32

Data Sample Period: Jan 2000 - Dec 2019

S.D. Rolling Beta = Standard deviation of rolling beta; Red = low period beta but high standard deviation

Table 9.2: The period betas for various asian hedge fund strategies (first row) against various systematic risk factors (first column) over the sample period January 2000 to December 2019

		Asia HF Index	Asia Arbitrage	Asia CTA/Managed Futures	Asia Fixed Income	Asia Long short equity	Asia Macro	Asia Multi Strategy	Asia Relative Value	Asia Distressed Debt	Asia Event Driven
SPX	Period Beta ('00-'19)	0.40	0.18	0.08	0.24	0.43	-0.05	0.24	0.27	0.14	0.29
	S.D. of Rolling Beta	0.13	0.13	0.18	0.20	0.14	0.20	0.12	0.20	0.13	0.18
USD	Period Beta ('00-'19)	-0.46	-0.18	-0.08	-0.48	-0.49	0.00	-0.34	-0.41	-0.24	-0.33
	S.D. of Rolling Beta	0.34	0.24	0.33	0.28	0.37	0.28	0.26	0.27	0.23	0.28
Commodity	Period Beta ('00-'19)	0.17	0.08	0.09	0.11	0.18	-0.01	0.11	0.12	0.10	0.12
	S.D. of Rolling Beta	0.12	0.09	0.11	0.14	0.13	0.10	0.10	0.11	0.08	0.12
Momentum	Period Beta ('00-'19)	-0.10	-0.07	-0.01	-0.05	-0.10	0.00	-0.02	-0.07	-0.02	-0.06
	S.D. of Rolling Beta	0.29	0.15	0.22	0.14	0.31	0.16	0.20	0.21	0.16	0.20
Value	Period Beta ('00-'19)	-0.18	-0.05	-0.22	-0.01	-0.20	0.25	-0.17	-0.03	0.01	-0.08
	S.D. of Rolling Beta	0.25	0.25	0.18	0.22	0.27	0.29	0.21	0.23	0.31	0.22
Credit	Period Beta ('00-'19)	-4.30	-2.01	-0.88	-4.64	-4.52	-0.76	-3.71	-3.59	-3.24	-4.14
	S.D. of Rolling Beta	4.09	2.11	6.21	3.19	4.56	4.61	2.36	3.11	3.60	4.10
Bond	Period Beta ('00-'19)	0.47	-0.01	1.12	-1.22	0.55	0.60	0.62	-0.30	0.54	0.78
	S.D. of Rolling Beta	3.32	2.15	3.03	2.89	3.55	1.96	2.34	3.00	3.45	3.54
DVIX	Period Beta ('00-'19)	-0.35	-0.18	-0.09	-0.23	-0.36	0.08	-0.23	-0.25	-0.15	-0.25
	S.D. of Rolling Beta	0.13	0.14	0.37	0.19	0.14	0.25	0.11	0.14	0.12	0.15
Size	Period Beta ('00-'19)	0.21	0.07	0.21	0.19	0.21	-0.11	0.29	0.12	0.11	0.15
	S.D. of Rolling Beta	0.30	0.29	0.18	0.28	0.31	0.20	0.24	0.25	0.28	0.31
Emerging Market	Period Beta ('00-'19)	0.36	0.15	0.09	0.21	0.38	0.03	0.26	0.23	0.14	0.24
	S.D. of Rolling Beta	0.07	0.08	0.13	0.13	0.08	0.12	0.06	0.16	0.08	0.12
Short Put	Period Beta ('00-'19)	0.48	0.20	0.14	0.31	0.51	-0.06	0.31	0.34	0.23	0.36
	S.D. of Rolling Beta	0.20	0.18	0.50	0.23	0.22	0.29	0.17	0.24	0.20	0.25

Data Sample Period: Jan 2000 - Dec 2019

S.D. Rolling Beta = Standard deviation of rolling beta; Red = low period beta but high standard deviation

changes in exposure over time. I provide results for Asian hedge fund strategies in addition to the usual North American strategies.

A summary of these results can be found in Tables 9.1 and 9.2.

Tables 9.1 and 9.2 include each hedge fund index strategy's regression beta from January 2000 to December 2019 against a systematic risk factor, which I refer to as the period beta.[1] I compare this against the standard deviation of the 24-month rolling betas over the same period.

A period beta value that is close to zero implies low average exposure to that particular risk factor. Since the bond and credit factors are based on yields, an absolute value that is less than one implies low average exposure. Additionally, due to the inverse relationship between bond prices and yields, a more negative beta for bond and credit implies increased market exposure. All other risk factors are based on total returns.

Overall, the period betas are low for both North American and Asian hedge fund index strategies, except — and understandably so — for some obvious ones, for example, a long–short equity's average positive exposure to the S&P 500 due to its long equity bias, various Asian hedge fund indexes' negative exposure to the USDX, and fixed income and debt strategies' high exposure to the credit factor.

Despite the low period betas, a more careful examination of the time series of the 24-month rolling beta, both by risk factor and hedge fund index strategy, revealed something slightly different.

9.3 Time Series Analysis

The entries highlighted in Tables 9.1 and 9.2 are those with low overall period betas, but which show significant deviation of the 24-month rolling betas when these values are plotted over time. A few strategies with large variation in factor exposures are highlighted below, first by systematic risk factors and then by hedge fund index strategies.

The first glaring observation was that exposures to several systematic factors on average have increased in recent years.

9.3.1 Increase in exposure to the S&P 500 factor

In 2017, Asia managed futures' rolling beta increased to 0.7 (Figure 9.1). In 2018, North American (NA) arbitrage increased to 0.5. Finally, in 2019, the rolling beta exposures of NA multi-strategy, NA distressed debt, and Asia event-driven increased to 0.6, 0.5, and 0.35, respectively.

---

[1] The average of the 24-month rolling betas is similar to the period beta over the sample period January 2000 to December 2019.

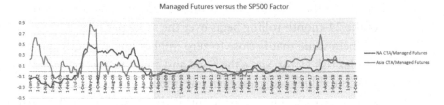

Figure 9.1: 24-month rolling beta for the managed futures hedge fund strategy against the S&P 500 factor

Data sample period: Jan 2000–Dec 2019; shaded in grey = post GFC period.

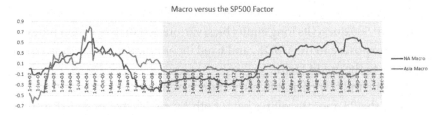

Figure 9.2: 24-month rolling beta for the macro hedge fund strategy against the S&P 500 factor

Data sample period: Jan 2000–Dec 2019; shaded in grey = post GFC period.

In the decade since the global financial crisis from 2009 to 2018, the beta exposure of NA macro on average steadily increased from minus 0.3 to 0.5 (Figure 9.2).

9.3.2 Increase in exposure to short put factor

Similarly, NA multi-strategy, NA macro, NA arbitrage, and NA event-driven indexes also showed a trend of increasing exposures to short put since 2008.

9.3.3 Increase in exposure to commodity factor

More recently, from 2018/2019 onwards, the NA and Asia hedge fund index (Figure 9.3), NA and Asia long–short equity, NA multi-strategy, NA distressed debt, NA macro, NA fixed income, NA and Asia relative value, and NA and Asia event-driven strategy indexes have shown an increase in beta to the commodity factor, from near zero to 0.3–0.5.

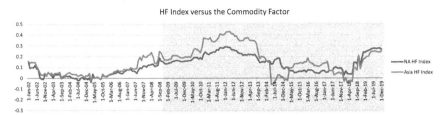

Figure 9.3:   24-month rolling beta for the hedge fund index strategy against the commodity factor

Data sample period: Jan 2000–Dec 2019; shaded in grey = post GFC period.

Comparing pre- and post-financial crisis exposures, NA distressed debt, NA and Asia event-driven, and NA and Asia relative value switched from negative to positive exposure.

However, one caveat is in order here. The correlations of commodity versus S&P 500 and other risk factors have increased post the financial crisis, which implies that the increased beta exposure may be a correlation effect.

9.3.4 Increase in exposure to credit spread factor

Exposure to credit has become more negative for most hedge fund index strategies between 2016 and 2020, indicating that a 1 percent increase/decrease in the credit spread led to a bigger decrease/increase in returns on average.

9.3.5 Increase in exposure to size factor

From 2018 to 2020, there was an overall increase in exposure to size for many hedge fund index strategies, as indicated by an increase in the rolling betas of North American and Asia hedge fund indexes (Figure 9.4), NA & Asia long–short equity, NA multi-strategy, NA distressed debt, NA macro, NA and Asia arbitrage, NA and Asia relative value, and NA and Asia event-driven against size.

9.3.6 Others

Other than the aforementioned factors, Asia distressed debt versus USDX increased from negative exposure to 0.25, while Asia arbitrage has increased

Figure 9.4:   24-month rolling beta for the hedge fund index strategy against the size factor
Data sample period: Jan 2000–Dec 2019; shaded in grey = post GFC period.

to 0.4 in recent years against the value factor. Since the financial crisis, Asia and NA event-driven have increased from an overall negative exposure to positive exposure against the value factor.

Finally, NA and Asia arbitrage, NA multi-strategy, and NA long–short equity have been showing increasing beta exposures against the emerging markets factor.

The 24-month rolling beta by hedge fund index strategy revealed similar glaring variations in beta across time that calls for attention.

9.4 North American Macro

The period beta of NA macro index ranges from minus 0.03 to 0.03 against the systematic total return risk factors, while it is between minus 0.29 and 0.81 for the yield factors (bond and credit). While almost all factor betas are close to zero, fluctuations in the 24-month rolling beta over time indicate this period average to be misleading.

For example, S&P 500 has 0.01 period beta, but rolling beta has been close to 0.5 since 2014. In fact, rolling beta was never totally zero, but positive before 2007, and approximately minus 0.25 from 2007 to 2013 (Figure 9.2). We observe the same pattern for the remaining factors, summarized in Table 9.3.

9.5 Asia Macro

Asia macro index shows a similar trend — period betas tend to be close to zero, except for value, size, and bond, which have betas greater than 0.1. However, fluctuations in the rolling betas indicate that beta is far from zero.

Table 9.3: NA Macro index strategy sample period beta versus rolling beta against various systematic factors

Factor	Period Beta	Rolling Beta Range and Comments
Short put	0.0	−0.5 to 1.3, beta steadily increases since 2013, peaking at 1.3 in 2018
Commodity	0.0	−0.2 to 0.2, 0.2 since 2018
Credit	0.81	−8 to +8
Bond	−0.29	−6 and +3
DVIX	0.01	−0.4 to +0.4
Size	−0.03	−0.5 to +0.5
Emerging markets	0.01	−0.15 to +0.3
Value	0.03	−0.6 to +0.6
Momentum	0.02	−0.4 to +0.6
USDX	−0.03	−0.6 to +0.5

Its fluctuation level is similar to NA macro, but there are periods where Asia macro beta shows sudden spikes that are much larger than NA macro.

A positive sign is that the variations in the betas for the macro strategy in general have become less extreme after the financial crisis.

9.6 Managed Futures

9.6.1 NA managed futures

With the exception of the USDX factor, the period beta of managed futures index is consistently close to zero for all factor betas, ranging between minus 0.01 and 0.06 for the total return factors, and minus 0.06 and 0.32 (bond and credit) for yield factors. However, a closer look at the rolling beta graphs shows significant time variation.

For example, S&P 500 showed a period beta of minus 0.01, but in fact, beta was 0.5 from 2004 to 2007, and fluctuated around 0.1 to 0.3 in recent years. We observe the same pattern for the remaining factors, summarized in Table 9.4.

9.6.2 Asia managed futures

Asia managed futures index showed a similar trend (Table 9.5).

Table 9.4: NA Managed Futures index strategy sample period beta versus rolling beta against various systematic factors

Factor	Period Beta	Rolling Beta Range and Comments
Credit	−0.32, indicating that 1 percent increase in credit spread leads to only 0.32 percent decrease in returns	−8 to +8
Bond	−0.06	−4 to +5
DVIX	−0.03	−0.5 to +0.3, positive (0.1 to 0.3) in the early 2000s and negative (−0.3 to −0.5) from 2005 to 2007
Emerging markets	0.03	−0.15 to +0.3, 0.15 since 2018
Value	0.05	−0.3 to +0.7
Short put	0.0	−0.2 to +0.8

Table 9.5: Asia Managed Futures index strategy sample period beta versus rolling beta against various systematic factors

Factor	Period Beta	Rolling Beta Range
S&P 500	0.08	−0.2 to +0.9
USDX	−0.08	−1.3 to +0.6
Momentum	−0.01	−0.3 to +0.9
Credit	−0.88	−17 to +11
DVIX	−0.09	−2.3 to +0.1

Similar to the macro strategy, variations in beta of managed futures have become less extreme post the financial crisis for S&P 500, USDX, value, commodity, momentum, DVIX, and emerging markets.

9.6.3 Others

In addition to macro and managed futures, several other hedge fund index strategies displayed low period beta but high volatility of rolling beta (Tables 9.1 and 9.2 highlighted in red) to momentum, bond, and value factors.

9.7 Conclusion

I have attempted to systematically categorize hedge fund index strategies' average and time series exposures to systematic risk factors, which are well accepted and established in academia and the industry. Along with my co-authors, I comprehensively compared 24-month rolling betas and average period betas of the various hedge fund index strategies, for both Asia and North America, against these risk factors.

While hedge fund strategies are on average worth their salt, the time series analysis shows that there is indeed still time variation to their "skill" in delivering alpha. The importance of due diligence in the hedge fund search process hence cannot be overemphasized.

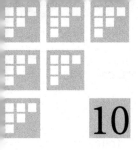

10

In Bonds We (Still) Trust*

Despite rock-bottom yields, debt remains important and relevant.

10.1 Introduction

Bonds have lost favour as an asset class as nominal yields of developed market debt slip into negative territory. They are expensive and do not generate sufficient income for those seeking a fixed income. While a low yield environment allows firms to borrow cheaply in capital markets, the role of bonds as the bedrock of asset–liability management in retirement portfolios is understandably being questioned.

10.2 The Function of Bonds

It's useful to step back and recall the function of bonds. As the typical bond fund would state in its prospectus, there is the issue of managing interest rate risk, credit risk, market risk, liquidity risk, country risk, foreign exchange risk, and in some cases, leverage. The two primary ways that bonds are utilized in investment portfolios are to generate income or return.

In liability-driven investing involving bonds, the portfolio would be structured to ensure it can meet current and future financial obligations. The income stream and return generated by the bond portfolio on the asset

---

* This chapter is excerpted from Asia Asset Management (2020). See Cherian and Yan (2020b).

side would be structured to meet its expense obligations on the liability side. Herein lies the problem. With yields at all-time lows, it's becoming more challenging for fund managers to generate the income stream needed by just using bonds.

In a total return portfolio including bonds, the maxim of diversification applies and the portfolio is managed to maximize risk–return trade-offs. Indeed, considering that yields have fallen, bond mutual funds and exchange-traded funds (ETFs) have had decent performance, delivering good risk-adjusted returns over the last 2 years. This "yield slide" is well captured by the bellwether 10-year US Treasury bond yield index (Figure 10.1).

As a consequence, the performance of certain global bond funds and ETFs has been comparable to that of corresponding equity funds. For example, over the past 2 years, the iShares Global Government Bond ETF has earned a respectable 12.04 percent, fairly close to the 12.47 percent earned by the iShares MSCI All Countries World Index ETF, while the latter has experienced much higher volatility (Figure 10.2).

In fact, given the lower volatility of bond funds, it's natural to compare the performance to a hedge fund index. As Figure 10.3 indicates, not only did the Eurekahedge Hedge Fund Index underperform both the iShares Global Government Bond ETF and the Vanguard Total Bond Market Index Fund over the last 2 years but the bond funds also delivered better returns at much lower volatility.

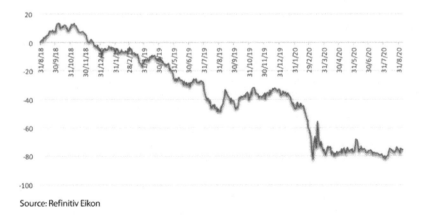

Source: Refinitiv Eikon

Figure 10.1: 10-year US treasury bond yield index (August 31, 2018–September 2, 2020)

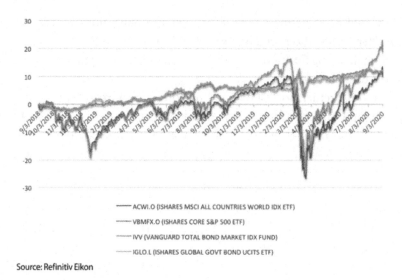

Source: Refinitiv Eikon

Figure 10.2: Various mutual fund and ETF performance (September 3, 2018–September 3, 2020)

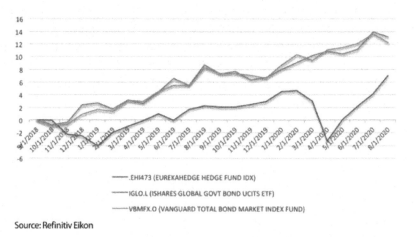

Source: Refinitiv Eikon

Figure 10.3: Hedge fund and bond mutual fund and ETF performance (%) (September 30, 2018–August 31, 2020)

In summary, it has not been all doom and gloom in the bond world after all. Note that we have abstracted away from credit risk, with spreads peaking around mid-March 2020 due to the coronavirus pandemic. But spreads have somewhat abated to almost pre-pandemic levels since then.

10.3 Liquidity

There is another aspect of bonds that is often overlooked — their role in the provision of liquidity. When dealers, banks, and market participants seek funding or liquidity, most of them go to the sovereign bond market, coupled with the repo market. In a 2004 theory paper titled *A Model of the Convenience Yields in On-the-run Treasuries*, one of us demonstrates how the most recently issued US Treasury bonds — also known as "on-the-run" securities — are the most liquid and actively traded. They are also most often used by institutional investors for hedging, speculation, delivery requirements in Treasury derivatives, and liquidity management purposes.[1]

This liquidity demand leads to the Treasury security trading "rich" in price — it is said to go on "special" — as compared to an otherwise identical Treasury that is not on special. The on-the-run Treasury is higher priced than the otherwise identical off-the-run Treasury because of the "dividend yield" effect that the former enjoys through lower borrowing cost associated with serving as collateral for financing in the repo market.

In fact, the term "convenience yield", which we first used in a related working paper from the late 1990s to describe the dividend yield effect of on-the-run Treasuries, is now commonplace in academic literature. This is a huge and important funding market in terms of daily volume; the Federal Reserve Bank of New York recently reported that the repo and reverse repo transactions against US government bonds outstanding are close to US$4 trillion, thus providing immense liquidity to the US financial market.

But, a word of caution here. We do not address the issue of liquidity drying up in corporates, such as the Franklin Templeton saga in India earlier this year, where the company shut down several bond mutual funds because of the seizure in Indian investment grade corporate bond liquidity triggered by the national lockdown to curb the spread of the coronavirus.

Closer to home, one of us also analysed Malaysian conventional and Islamic government bonds for repo trading effects.[2] Malaysia has the largest and most active Islamic bond market in the world, with demand from both conventional and Islamic investors; the latter group is mandated to only hold Islamic debt.

We document that Malaysian Islamic sovereigns have a 4.8 basis point higher yield than their conventional counterparts. This spread is due to foreign institutional investors participating more actively in the conventional market than in the Islamic market.

10.4 The Role of Bond Repo in Increasing Liquidity

More interestingly, Malaysian conventional sovereigns have an active repo market with higher bond "specialness", which allows market participants to benefit from holding the conventional bonds as special collateral for financing, as in the case of US "on-the-run" Treasuries. This causes them to trade "rich" relative to their Malaysian sovereign Islamic counterparts.

Our research indicates that the average yield spread between these two types of otherwise identical Malaysian sovereign bonds widens because of the conventionals trading rich when serving as special collateral in the repo market. More specifically, we document Malaysian sovereign Islamic bonds having up to 17.5 basis points higher yield — implying a lower bond price — than their conventional counterparts because of the specialness conventionals obtain from repo markets.

10.5 Convertible Securities

Finally, a hybrid form of bond, namely, a convertible bond, receives a coupon rate that is typically lower than its straight bond counterpart. At the same time, it offers the option to convert the bond into a predetermined number of shares of the underlying stock.

Investing in convertible bonds is meaningful in several ways. First, it provides strong downside protection. If the company does not default on its bond payments, investors' invested capital or principal is protected. In more technical terms, they will get their "par" value back.

Second, if the company's stock price appreciates significantly, convertible bond investors also own a call option on the underlying stock, which is unlike traditional bonds. They are hence able to significantly participate in the stock's upside.

Third, convertible bonds have seniority over shareholders in the capital structure. Fourth, many convertible issuers tend to be in the technology, healthcare, and consumer sectors, thus allowing investors to participate in the growth of these sectors while managing downside risk.

Compared with owning straight equities, investors are giving up some of the upside while gaining downside protection. Such an asymmetric risk–reward payoff works especially well during volatile markets. Figure 10.4 demonstrates the year-to-date returns of the Refinitiv Global Focus Convertible Bond Index versus various equity indices.

From the issuer's point of view, convertible bonds allow the company to monetize its volatility, hence lowering its borrowing cost. The dilution effect from the stock option embedded in the convertible bond will only come into play when the stock has significantly appreciated. For example, during Amazon's early years, when the company had yet to generate any profits, it successfully used multiple large convertible issuances to help it weather "growing pains" and the dot-com crash.

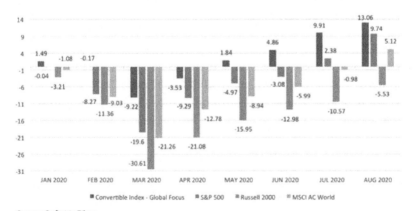

Source: Refinitiv Eikon

Figure 10.4: Convertible index versus equity indices YTD % performance (January 1, 2020–August 31, 2020)

Source: Calamos Investments

Figure 10.5:   Valuation of the convertible market (June 30, 1995–July 31, 2020)

So why aren't more people invested in convertible bonds now? Part of the reason is because they are complex hybrid securities that combine characteristics of bonds, stocks, and call options. Their valuations are thus impacted by changes in interest rates, credit ratings, and the underlying stock prices. Figure 10.5 depicts the overall cheapness or richness of the convertible market annually for the past 25 years.

10.6 Conclusion

The multi-functional nature of bonds, especially in the convertible bond and vast repo funding market, demonstrates the importance and relevance of bonds to the real economy and to both financial and non-financial firms, even when yields are collapsing around us. So, it's not yet time to write off bonds.

11

In Bonds We (Still) Trust: Part 2*

Convertible bonds may be a conservative way to participate in volatile markets.

11.1 Introduction

In the earlier chapter, I argued against writing off bonds just because yields are in low territory. This is due to bonds having a multi-functional role in capital markets: in the provision of liquidity, preservation of capital, and, indeed, in the supply of income, at least in the case of higher-yielding corporate and convertible bonds.

In this chapter, we shall focus purely on convertible bonds.

11.2 Hybrid Security

A convertible bond is a hybrid security. It looks like a plain vanilla corporate bond, meaning it bears a maturity date, coupon payment, face value, and credit risk. However, it also includes an option to convert into a predetermined number of shares of the common stock of the underlying company.

Consequently, a convertible security's unique nonlinear hybrid payoff structure is equivalent to a call option and a bond (or a put option and

*This chapter is excerpted from Asia Asset Management (2021). See Cherian and Yan (2021).

equity if appealing to put-call parity) — it provides a bond floor in bad times and equity participation in good.

Convertible bonds may provide a conservative way for investors to participate in the equity market in the current volatile environment, with market prognosticators predicting a "risk-on" situation from the expected early cycle economic recovery in 2021. The pundits nevertheless still have an eye on potential downside risks from global economic fragility stemming from unfinished trade wars, deglobalization, deranged political leaders, and a prolonged coronavirus pandemic.

To the extent that the equity and credit markets have already priced in any slower growth and the uncertainties ahead, a rebound in the underlying equity and credit would both benefit convertible bonds.

On the other hand, in case the equity market weakens, the bond feature of the convertible will ease the downside risk. Should the credit deteriorate further, and the company go into bankruptcy, convertible holders would have a senior claim before equity shareholders.

11.3 Current Valuation

In addition, many convertible bonds are trading below their theoretical fair value, i.e., they are cheap based on valuation. According to Calamos Investments (Figure 11.1), the ICE BofA All US Convertible Index was

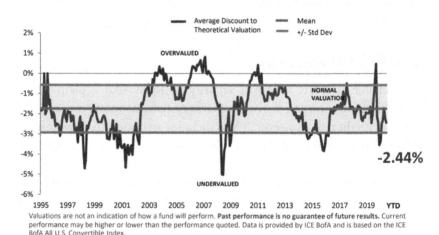

Figure 11.1:   Valuation of the convertible market (June 30, 1995–November 30, 2020)
Source: Calamos Investments.

trading at an average discount of minus 2.44 percent to theoretical value in November 2020.

This phenomenon is not unique to US convertible bonds. Chinese computer maker Lenovo, which issued US$675 million of 5-year convertible bonds with a 3.75 percent coupon on January 24, 2019, is also seeing the debt trade cheap currently. According to Refinitiv, it was quoted at a minus 3.97 percent discount to fair value in late December 2020.

11.4 Benefits

In summary, all things being equal and cheapness aside, investing in convertibles balances investors' need to protect their capital and receive periodic coupons, while not foregoing the potential equity upside. All this is accomplished via a single hybrid security, which would normally take a portfolio of the underlying equity and derivatives to achieve the same effect.

Unlike a straight equity or bond, the trading character of convertible bonds is different in an up versus down market. And it changes dynamically to the advantage of investors. When the market is advancing, the bonds become like equity, because the option to convert becomes increasingly in the money. When the market is declining, it behaves like a bond, because the face value is promised to be returned to investors at maturity.

This hedging-like feature allows investors to obtain greater downside protection while maintaining the upside potential. Over time, the asymmetric up/down market behaviour leads to returns like those of stocks but with a lower volatility. Thus, it is common to see mutual funds, insurance firms, and retirement funds among the long-only investors in convertibles.

Furthermore, while convertible bond returns have lower volatility, the volatility of the underlying equity of the company translates to a welcome positive. This is because the option to convert is increasingly valuable as the underlying volatility increases. Indeed, this is partly why convertibles are usually issued by start-ups, technology firms, venture funds, and other firms that have highly volatile payoff structures.

On the issuer side, before Amazon became the powerhouse it is today, capital infusion through two convertible bond offerings in 1999 and 2000 helped it weather the dotcom crash of 2000, which wiped out more than

90 percent of its stock price in a 2-year period. Amazon was able to raise capital at a coupon rate lower than its straight debt, while convertible investors received 4.75 percent and 6.90 percent in coupon payments versus stockholders who received zero dividends until the stock price recovered.

As mentioned, convertible investors have seniority over equity holders in the event of bankruptcy; convertibles rank higher than stocks in the capital structure pecking order of the firm.

11.5 Complexity

But buyer beware. Due to their hybrid nature, the relative value of convertibles as well as the trading behaviour is highly complex and contingent upon many moving parts, such as the underlying equity price, credit spread, interest rates, volatility, and the "Greeks", like delta, gamma, and theta (time decay). Figures 11.2 and 11.3 depict the complex nature of convertible bond valuation and evolution at both individual security and index levels.

For yield-seeking investors, convertibles typically have lower income streams than the corresponding bonds, as in the case of Amazon. In addition, the advantage of downside protection with upside potential comes with a cost, called conversion premium, which is the amount by which the price of a convertible security exceeds the current market value of the common stock into which it may be converted at a point in time. They may also have embedded features such as being callable, i.e., the issuing company may "call back" the security, thus limiting the upside when you most need it.

However, converting the securities can be highly dilutive to existing shareholders if it does not have any anti-dilution provisions or clauses.

Finally, convertibles may not be accessible to some investors due to the minimum investment size, liquidity, and credit rating, among other things. That said, there are funds and exchange-traded funds that provide such investors access to a diversified set of convertible bonds.

11.6 Asia Markets

At the macro level, Asia's relative economic strength provides many growth opportunities. We have already seen the flow of funds shift weight from

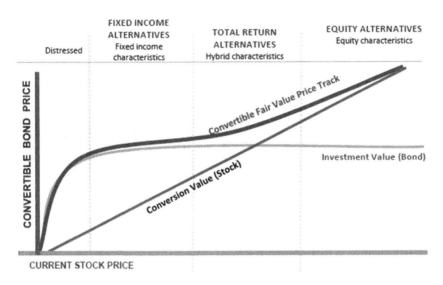

Figure 11.2:   Convertible bond valuation

Source: Calamos Investments.

Figure 11.3:   Refinitiv convertible index — Asia focus (USD, Hedged)

Sample period: 7 Jan 2011–1 Jan 2021 (Weekly).

Notes:

▬▬▬▬▬ Asia Focus Convertible Index Values (USD, Hedged).

▬▬▬▬ Average Premium (or conversion premium, which is the difference between the convertible price and current equity price).

▬▬▬▬▬ Average Delta (sensitivity of the convertible price to the underlying equity price).

Source: Refinitiv.

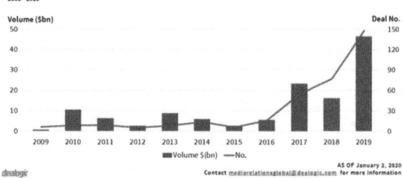

Figure 11.4:   Deal volumes in USD in the Chinese A-share convertible bond market (2009–2019)
Source: Dealogic.

the West to East as this region's growth continues. Increasingly larger issues of convertible bonds are coming from Asia, such as China's Daqin Railway, which sold US$4.89 billion of 6-year convertibles with a 0.2 percent coupon on December 10. As Asia accounts for an increasingly larger share of new securities issuance globally, convertible issuance will also rise.

Asia's bond markets are still in their infancy in many markets, including China. Yet, China is the second largest bond market in the world after the US. According to Dealogic, China had a record US$46.5 billion of convertibles in 148 issuances in 2019 (Figure 11.4).

The World Bank ranks Malaysia third in Asia in terms of bond market development. The combined size of Malaysia's *sukuk* or Islamic bond and conventional bond markets is approximately 98 percent of the country's gross domestic product.[1]

In general, the development of the traditional bond market in Asia will be crucial for the development of its convertible bond market.

11.7 Hedge Community and Conclusion

The convertible "hedge" community was a significant part of the market before the coronavirus crisis. They typically long convertibles and short

---

[1] World Bank. 2020. Malaysia's Domestic Bond Market: A Success Story. World Bank, Washington, DC. URL: https://openknowledge.worldbank.org/handle/10986/34538.

the underlying stock or credit, to take advantage of cheap borrowing costs, cheap volatility (implying lower valuation), or the income advantage over stocks.

As the cost of borrowing and leveraging becomes unfavourable, the hedge communities may become less active. Long-only investors focus more on the underlying company's health and growth thesis. As the underlying stock and credit become cheaper and long-only positions become more profitable, we should see the investor base tilt towards the long-only or "outright" investors.

Over time, we expect both the hedge community and the outright community to be active participants of the global convertible bond market, including in Asia.

Part 2

Infrastructure Finance, Digital Currency, Disruption, and New Economy

12

Making Infrastructure Assets More Palatable: A Unified Market Approach to Infrastructure Financing*

12.1 Introduction

The gulf between sanctioned infrastructure projects in Asia, estimated at US$730 billion per year in 2018, and the available infrastructure funding, at 10 percent of this number, speaks for itself. The public sector currently finances over 90 percent of Asia's infrastructure investments, and as infrastructure demand continues to grow, more private funding will be required to plug the gap.

A unique solution is required. One based on a global approach, combining cutting-edge techniques in valuation, structured finance, and capital markets, where an intermediation role can be effectively played by the financial centres of the world.

12.2 Approach to Valuation

The first problem facing infrastructure finance is accurate valuation. Proper valuation of infrastructure assets requires that scale, uncertainty,

---

*This chapter is excerpted from *Asia Asset Management*, May 2018, Vol 23, No. 5. See Chakravarty *et al.* (2018).

environmental impact, embedded flexibilities, and externalities — both positive and negative — be considered and adequately priced.

A realistic and appealing approach to valuation is real options analysis (ROA), which incorporates uncertainty and stock market-like volatility measures to eliminate biases in traditional capital budgeting that lead to mispricing or underpricing of infrastructure projects — directly affecting the "bankability" of such projects. We dive deeper into real options analysis (ROA), which can be used for project feasibility and due diligence studies, in the next chapter.

12.3 Tools for the Job

ROA valuation models can also be applied to project guarantees and project bonds with coupons, be it immediate or deferred. Additionally, pooling underlying real assets, such as toll roads, then matching up their cash flows and adding a credit enhancement facility, results in a classic infrastructure asset-backed security.

A paradigm shift is also needed. Many investors may only accept "plain vanilla" assets, or structures which they can easily understand, while others may be more sophisticated or managing a rapidly growing portfolio. Between these extremes, repackaging the different structures and credit enhancements to create asset classes or investment products can meet the different needs of investors.

One example is the Managed Co-lending Portfolio Programme (MCPP) of the International Finance Corporation (IFC), the private sector arm of the World Bank. The programme enables asset owners and managers to participate in IFC's future loan portfolio with due diligence conducted by experts on the ground. The MCPP allows investors to piggyback off IFC's expertise in locating, managing, and syndicating bankable emerging market infrastructure projects, offers them within a portfolio context at a scale that is both well diversified and low cost, and provides for a credit enhancement component, which enables more institutional investors to participate.

There is also a shortage of transparent data that can validate the expected returns of infrastructure, and a dearth of operational players that effectively marry the financial and engineering aspects of infrastructure projects to "crowd-in" private sector investment.

To this end, Singapore-based infrastructure consultancy company Surbana Jurong (SJ) has teamed up with the Asian Development Bank-linked Credit Guarantee & Investment Facility (CGIF) to support its construction period guarantee product. With its Association of Southeast Asian Nations (ASEAN) operating knowledge, SJ's validation of time, cost, and quality aspects of selected greenfield infrastructure lends assurance to the CGIF's issuance of local currency-denominated project bond guarantees.

This de-risks infrastructure projects by eliminating foreign currency exposure for the issuer and providing investors with the necessary assurance to invest in Southeast Asian greenfield bonds.

12.4 Defining Infrastructure

Developing a strong pipeline requires good asset ownership, asset management, and investible capital. The sovereign in whose jurisdiction the asset is located needs to be assured, while the asset manager who structures the asset's finances on the sell-side and books it on the buy-side must be competent.

Global financial hubs must facilitate seamless movement of investible capital into and out of infrastructure assets to encourage the origination, structuring, trading, and liquidity in this asset class.

A precedent for an uncertain cash flow-based asset with tax advantages and a long and profitable history already exists in the form of real estate investment trust (REIT) structures. Backed by a sovereign guarantee, an infrastructure investment trust could be similarly attractive.

12.5 Role of Long-term Savings

One critical missing piece in infrastructure financing is the availability of long-term savings in local currencies to match the financing needs of long-term projects. Servicing foreign currency debt is untenable to project companies and economies — a lesson learnt in the 1997–98 Asian financial crisis.

Possible measures include allowing mandatory retirement saving schemes to capture the "demographic dividends" of emerging economies, as Malaysia's Employees Provident Fund does.

Reforms to the life insurance sector to promote traditional life insurance products, rather than investment-linked insurance products, would provide insurers with the discretion to invest in more complex, long-term project finance.

Long-term savings are conservative and expected to provide stable returns. Mobilizing these savings into infrastructure projects via project bonds requires transparent market regulations, adequate bond structuring skills, robust national ratings framework, and innovative credit enhancement products.

Well-run sovereign-backed and multilateral guarantors play a role in building confidence by absorbing project risks that are not yet well understood in the marketplace. This would make project bonds with credit enhancements a prime asset class.

Private sector guarantors, and the global reinsurers behind them, can supplement the capacities of the national and multilateral institutions, and together crowd-in other private sector participants.

12.6 Exchange and Clearing

The remaining need is for a credible counterparty in infrastructure-backed securities, as in the case for high-yield bonds or REITs. This is where the exchange and clearing corporation enters the picture as a guarantor of settlement, a source of price discovery, and as an avenue for the provision of liquidity of infrastructure project bonds.

The exchange's listing facility is the avenue for the infrastructure asset to go through an initial public offering for early investor exit, infusion of capital for speculation and investment, and first-stage systemic risk insulation.

The appointments of clearing members, market makers, and trading members all drive the basics of liquidity provision.

In the paradigm shift from multiple over-the-counter structures housed in various institutions in multiple jurisdictions, globally regarded exchanges similarly play a crucial role beyond clearing and settlement for infrastructure finance.

Given that infrastructure product structures involve significant interest rates and other risks, the existence of major swap warehousing facilities contiguous with these assets offers not only products for investors and traders to benefit from but also measures for the clearing corporation to manage its market risk.

Natural diversification and risk management would serve to strengthen the clearing corporation organically, enhancing its value as a central counterparty to the asset owner and manager.

12.7 Role of Ratings Agencies

In an ideal world, Moody's Investors Service, Standard & Poor, and Fitch Ratings would be actively involved in the rating of infrastructure asset structures. These ratings would be published and proper records maintained; for local currency financing fulfilled by long-term local savings, national-scale ratings, and robust analysis and standards, are crucial to pitch the asset class as safe and stable for long-term investors.

Historical transactions and trading data need to be reported, captured, and preserved in real time. The US's Trade Reporting and Compliance Engine (TRACE), Malaysia's Bond Info Hub, and the China Foreign Exchange Trade System (CFETS) are good cases in point.

Such preservation of quality transactions and trade data allows for in-depth research to be conducted, improving price transparency and liquidity. Ancillary primary and derivative products for the investing community can also be derived.

12.8 Infrastructure Ecosystem

The most important issue facing the infrastructure asset class is recourse in the unforeseen event of failure. This necessitates that the exchange and clearing house should be in a jurisdiction with impeccable legal processes and mechanisms.

A supportive ecosystem that provides seamless connectivity and zero failure in power systems, information flow, and connectivity is also required.

In addition, the exchange's jurisdiction should have access to cutting-edge capital market talent, with financial technology enabling innovation, productivity gains, and cost reduction in financial intermediation.

Last but not least, the infrastructure ecosystem and value chain need to be lean, green, and clean, to quote the China-led Asian Infrastructure Investment Bank. Infrastructure decision-making, investments, and issuance have to be environmentally friendly, socially responsible, and good governance practicing, where the actors have the fiduciary responsibility of serving the best interests of all stakeholders and beneficiaries involved.

12.9 Conclusion

In summary, a precise commercial roadmap for making infrastructure assets more palatable and tradable is needed. It will not be long before a global financial hub steps up to the plate, provides the necessary ecosystem, and potentially dominates this highly lucrative asset class.

13

Infrastructure Financing*

Without oversimplifying, the appeal of infrastructure assets is the steady, predictable, and long-term nature of their cash flows. These features adequately meet the asset and liability needs of sovereign funds, insurance companies, and pension plans which are constantly looking for alternative sources of risk premia (and hence returns) in this low-yield interest rate environment. Over the last 5 to 10 years, the FTSE Global Core Infrastructure Index of infrastructure-related listed securities worldwide returned 6.5 percent and 6.1 percent per annum, while the EDHECinfra's most representative index of unlisted infrastructure equity, the infra300 Index, returned 5.03 percent and 13.5 percent per annum, respectively. U.S. President Joe Biden has been the latest leader to jump on the infrastructure bandwagon, with a US$2.3 trillion spending plan, around 50 percent of which is estimated to go towards physical infrastructure, such as rebuilding roads and bridges.

13.1 The Case of Singapore: Rethinking Infrastructure Finance

Singapore, too, has been at the forefront of infrastructure financing and development through Infrastructure Asia, a government agency which partners with various stakeholders for this purpose in Southeast and

---

* This chapter is excerpted from the *Nomura Journal of Asian Capital Markets*, Autumn 2021, Vol. 6, No. 1. See Cherian (2021).

South Asia. Additionally, Singapore boasts some of the region's leaders in infrastructure development, particularly in urban planning, design, and build. These include Surbana Jurong and Sembcorp.

I would like to explore three areas as new ways to think about investing in infrastructure. They are the use of real options analysis (ROA) for project feasibility and due diligence studies; the innovative financing opportunities available in urban infrastructure in this region from the "value-chain solution provider's" point of view, especially focusing on green and sustainability financing initiatives in urban infrastructure; and the potential of digital security token issuance to enable broader participation of non-accredited investors in the real economy. In other words, giving smaller investors the opportunity to invest in infrastructure.

First, ROA, which, unlike traditional capital budgeting using the ubiquitous discounted cash flow (DCF) model, takes uncertainty and flexibility into consideration when evaluating whether projects add value. ROA incorporates the impact of risk and uncertainty in irreversible investment projects, while explicitly valuing the inherent flexibilities in project management along the way, including project deferment, abandonment, or expansion. In a Surbana Jurong Capital test case study conducted in 2020 involving a wind farm within this region, students at the National University of Singapore (NUS) Business School divided the project into the following three irreversible stages (financial stages in parenthesis): feasibility studies (due diligence), project structuring and engineering (deal structuring), and construction (actual financing starts). A critical result from the study is that the difference in net present value of the project using the DCF versus ROA method increases monotonically in ROA's favour as the volatility of the future cash flows to the project increases. The intuition behind this result is that in the ROA approach, the model considers the project manager's ability, or flexibility, to abandon, defer, expand, or re-contract. As financial option pricing theory predicts, the higher the volatility (or uncertainty) of the underlying project's future cash flows, the greater this project's "flexibility" premium.[1]

---

[1] A caveat is in order here. While ROA provides a better returns representation of the project given it reflects the added optionality and risk premium, the corresponding challenge is the accuracy of both the underlying assumptions and ascertainment of the parameters associated with the ROA methodology.

Second is a new way of thinking about urban infrastructure financing that offers the opportunity to promote green and sustainable goals. In November 2020, the MAS launched the world's first Green and Sustainability-Linked Loan Grant Scheme for corporates. The financing scheme is such that independent service providers can be engaged by corporates, particularly SMEs, to validate that loan proceeds are used for green and sustainable purposes. So, why don't the industry and policymakers allow for green, sustainability, and social-linked home mortgage schemes too, especially in the case of affordable housing? Any housing project — and its residents — that supports the Sustainable Development Goals (SDGs), environment, social, and governance (ESG), circular economy, renewable energy and energy efficient activities, biological diversity, or which minimizes the social and environmental footprint, as well as promoting sustainable food/farming practices, would qualify for this Green and Social-linked Home Mortgage Scheme. Or the developer could offer a green-linked rent-to-own scheme, which combines a standard lease agreement with an option to buy before the lease terminates.

13.2 Transformation, Disruption, and Digitization

Finally, on the digital front, tremendous strides have been taken in Singapore to allow the issuance of digital securities, both traditional bonds and private equity-backed bonds, and digital token securities for the trading and settlement of the same in smaller denominations.

In the former case, HSBC Singapore and Marketnode (a joint Singapore Exchange (SGX) and Temasek digital asset issuance, depository, and servicing platform) have recently completed a digital bond issuance process in conjunction with a traditional bond issue from Singtel. According to HSBC Singapore, digital bond issuance is achieved by creating a "distributed ledger technology electronic platform that connects various parties in bond issuances and uses self-executing smart contracts to automate processes such as issuance flows and coupon payments." In other words, a blockchain system.

In the latter case, a Temasek portfolio company, Azalea Investment Management, has been issuing listed bonds on a diversified portfolio of private equity funds held by Temasek, commencing in 2016 with Astrea III. The latest in the series of such PE-backed bonds, Astrea VI, is now witnessing local digital asset exchange, iSTOX, issuing tokens on Astrea VI. The tokenized offering of such bonds, down to a minimum size of US$20,000, allows for "fractionalized ownership" of Temasek's PE funds, giving greater access to a broader range of investors, as well as better after-market liquidity for those who need it.

A similar strong case can also be made for digital issuance and tokenization of infrastructure finance securities, so that a broader swath of investors can participate and benefit from the growth in the real economy through infrastructure investment.

13.3 Conclusion

In this introductory treatise on infrastructure finance, I have shown that the ROA approach in infrastructure finance adds value over and above traditional capital budgeting using discounted cash flows. ROA provides for the necessary trade-off and opportunity cost analysis that stems from the ability of the decision maker to adapt to changing scenarios in real time, be they economic, environmental, regulatory, social, or political. And what kind of stewards are we if our decision-making in this space is not green and sustainable? Furthermore, innovations in home mortgage financing and leasing can promote green and sustainable goals, while innovations in digital securities issuance can promote access to a broader range of participants. Rethinking the roles of financial markets, innovation, and government policy in retirement finance, SME financing and infrastructure financing in the ways described here will strengthen resilience in the face of future systemic crises, in Singapore and around the world.

14

Oh, Behave! Why the AIIB Can Be a Win for China and Asia: Can China Bring Its Mojo to the World of Infrastructure Financing?

"Oh, behave!" That's how Austin Powers, the alpha male, James Bond-like "man of mystery" would put any misbehaving sidekicks in their place. In a world with badly behaved players in the Eurozone, the South China Sea, Eastern Europe, and many other hotspots of the world, Mr. Powers' rebuke, "Oh, Behave!" could not be more timely.

14.1 Introduction

The formal launch in 2015 of the Asian Infrastructure Investment Bank (AIIB), which is primarily dominated by China, may have the appearance of "rivalling" the World Bank (primarily dominated by the US) and the Asian Development Bank (primarily dominated by Japan). But the truth that is the demand for infrastructure financing in Asia far exceeds the supply of funds available from the traditional multilateral lenders.

The funds are needed to finance the building of highways, power plants, dams, ports, and airports. Asian countries such as India, Indonesia, Myanmar, and Vietnam are in dire need of infrastructure funding — hence the relevance and timeliness of the AIIB.

As I argue in Cherian (2015b), China undeniably has made some incredible strides on the infrastructure front, with state-of-the-art airports, cities, ports, and high-speed trains. In its quest to build new growth drivers for its economy, it would like to export some of the homegrown infrastructure technologies and expertise to the rest of Asia.

However, China's forays into overseas infrastructure projects in Asia and Africa have been accompanied by accusations of corruption, lack of transparency, and questionable standards of governance.

14.2 Governance and Transparency

That is not to say that current multilateral lenders from the West are paragons of virtue when it comes to infrastructure projects. They, too, have had their fair share of colossal failures.

As a consequence, the AIIB should be welcomed, rather than obstructed — as the U.S. and Japanese governments have foolishly appeared to be doing since Day One. Indeed, despite their efforts, 57 countries signed the articles of association creating the AIIB's legal framework by the end of 2015, and the AIIB has since grown to 104 members.

The hope or expectation is that China, as the largest shareholder in the AIIB, will behave in a statesman-like manner commensurate with its status as the world's second largest and most interesting economy. That would be a win–win situation for all involved in infrastructure projects and their funding, one which emphasizes good governance, transparency, and above-board bidding schemes.

All the better if the AIIB — as the new kid on the multilateral development bank block and a vehicle for Chinese leadership — can establish a better process for implementing much-needed infrastructure projects in an effective and efficient manner. That would benefit Asia but would also push other players to raise their game.

Developed Southeast Asian countries like Singapore, in this respect, could also play a role. Singapore has the potential to further develop its infrastructure ecosystem to serve as a hub for innovative project development and finance in the Southeast Asia and broader Asian region. Indeed, Singapore-based financial entities, as of 2015, were already conducting some 70 percent of the ongoing infrastructure and project finance within this region.

14.3 Trade, Talent, and Knowledge

As in the development of other industry hubs, Singapore could capitalize on its reputation as a global centre of trade, talent, and knowledge as well as its geographical proximity to China, India, and the Southeast Asian region, which has a rapidly growing need for infrastructure.

In addition, Singapore enjoys strong engineering capabilities, financial hub status, and a good legal and regulatory system. It also has the ability to integrate all these elements for the benefit of infrastructure projects.

As a consequence, an initiative to develop an infrastructure ecosystem in Singapore would be a high value-add to the industry, with the potential to employ new finance techniques that take advantage of extant tax treaties and structures to reduce the cost of capital.

That was probably why Singapore has been given a high-profile role in the AIIB, with a key summit meeting co-chaired by China and Singapore to establish the AIIB's articles of association being held in Singapore in May of 2015.

Our universities can also play a role by developing a resource base and network that will nurture linkages between academia, private sector companies, the financial services industry, and governments when implementing projects in private infrastructure finance. They can equip the public and private sectors, as well as sponsor organizations, with the skills needed to deal with the complexities of infrastructure finance.

Education and thought leadership are key components in facilitating the development and documentation of new infrastructure financing and structuring models that could reduce the cost of capital, as happened with the advent of REITs in real estate finance.

Last but not least, Singapore's experience and involvement in the AIIB and associated infrastructure projects can help mitigate corruption, promote good governance, and ensure that high-quality infrastructure standards are maintained.

14.4 Conclusion

There is much to do in the infrastructure space. In a previous chapter, I already discussed the importance of both infrastructure assets and the innovative financial structures needed to support them. There's much to be done, especially with respect to securing our cities and societies from the ravages of natural disasters, be they climate change induced or otherwise. The key to our infrastructure development success is doing these projects right, where slogans like *lean, clean, and green* are not just hollow claims, but meaningful calls to action about keeping things above board. That way, no one will need to use the Austin Powers "Oh, behave!" admonition.

15

On the Role of Blockchain in Democratizing the Investment Opportunity Set

One of the key functions of capital markets is to enable investors, savers, and other market participants to enjoy the benefits of efficiently transferring risks, seeking long-term returns, and hence participating in and facilitating economic growth. I therefore find it curious that some countries' regulators place inadvertent roadblocks or hurdles that prevent investors from easily achieving those goals. Cases in point:

a. Requiring investors to take assessment or knowledge tests to invest in low-cost, well-diversified ETF strategies, whereas there may be no such requirement when buying risky, single-company stocks and shares in, say, the energy sector.
b. Disallowing non-accredited investors from accessing the more lucrative alternative investments sector, even if offered in small bite-sized chunks.

In this chapter, we will explore how financial technology has made access to financial markets and products more equitable and cost efficient.

15.1 Introduction

Technology has predominantly been the great equalizer, the transformative force that levels the playing field for participants in a particular industry, as well as in reducing the associated costs. To a certain extent, blockchain technology has been levelling the playing field in the financial industry.

Indeed, stock market-led riches have been deluding the masses in a major way until more recently. This had led to the *Matthew Effect*, a term which was coined by one of 20th century's most renowned sociologists, Professor Robert K. Merton, to demonstrate that the rich were not just getting richer but disproportionately so. A 2020 Gallup poll in the U.S. found that some 55 percent of households owned stocks. In Japan, the number is closer to 20 percent. The bulk of a high-net-worth investor's wealth, usually accumulated over a number of years, is often made up of a combination of both traditional asset classes, such as equities and bonds, and alternative assets, such as hedge funds, private equity, and real estate funds.

The latter asset class set has traditionally been out of reach of retail investors. The argument usually given by regulators and financial authorities is that investing in alternatives requires sophisticated investment skills and understanding. However, the advent of technology, particularly security tokens issued via blockchain, may change that.

15.2 Blockchain: The Road to Riches

In an article by Cherian and Cokeng (2019c), we assert that blockchain, via its distributed ledger technology and associated electronic platforms, will enable smaller denominations of "complex" securities, such as alternative investments, to be offered in a digital format, not dissimilar to cryptocurrencies. The main difference with cryptos will be that digital security tokens are collateralized by the underlying alternative asset. A case in point would be allowing the issuance, trading, and settlement of digital tokens on bonds and private equity-backed bonds in smaller denominations, as Singapore recently did.

Indeed, HSBC Singapore and Marketnode, as discussed in a previous chapter, announced the issuance of digital bonds in conjunction with a traditional bond issue from Singtel.

In the case of Azalea Investment Management's series of Astrea private equity (PE) bonds, the underlying asset is a diversified portfolio of Temasek's private equity funds. The issuance of Astrea VI saw iSTOX getting into the action by issuing tokens on Astrea VI in March 2021, down to a minimum denomination of US$20,000. In other words, it gives investors "fractionalized ownership" in Temasek's PE funds, as well as after-market liquidity for such digitized securities through iSTOX's secondary trading, custody, and settlement facility.

Given this digitization path with respect to corporate bonds and PE bonds, why not extend this notion to the digital issuance and tokenization of infrastructure finance securities as well? In this way, citizens as investors can participate and benefit from the real growth in the nation's economy, which is best reflected through its infrastructure investments.

15.3 Security Tokens are Like Fractionalized Asset-backed Securities

We point out in our 2019 article that Modern Portfolio Theory informs us that diversification improves the risk–reward trade-off frontier for investors. The lower the correlation between asset classes, the better looking the frontier. Yet, some of the fastest-growing asset classes, including private equity and hedge funds, are excluded from many investors' investment opportunity set. This is because many investors, firstly, do not fall within the "accredited investors" category, which means you are both wealthy and a super-sophisticated investor. Secondly, the minimum ticket sizes and fees are fairly large, hence posing as barriers to entry for less wealthy and less sophisticated investors.

We argue in the essay that need not be the case. Digital security tokens that are (a) backed by underlying alternative assets and securities, such as real estate, infrastructure assets, private equity funds, and bonds, (b) appropriately fractionalized, and (c) made tradable on a digital exchange, can lead to much wider access and hence greater liquidity, diversification, and risk-adjusted returns for smaller investors, too.

The key to all this is blockchain technology, which can create fractional, tradable digital ownership structures collateralized by assets and securities whose ownership is recorded on a secure distributed ledger platform and traded on an associated electronic trading exchange.

Apart from improving risk/reward characteristics, security tokens become more attractive when the underlying assets are products of high-quality issuers, proper due diligence, and perhaps even coupled with ESG principles. This is partly the reason why Temasek's PE-backed Astrea bonds are often oversubscribed when offered to retail investors. Temasek is considered a high-quality investor with a strong sustainability focus and reputation.

If security tokens and their underlying assets are of a financial nature, we would expect them to be regulated no differently from traditional financial securities. Issuers, brokers, and exchanges need to also ensure that all the proper Know Your Customer (KYC) and Anti-money Laundering (AML) compliance protocols have been adhered to when investors buy and trade them. The digital platforms and exchanges hosting such tokens, such as iSTOX, typically use the latest financial technology to ensure a smooth on-boarding process for the investor and technologically driven trading experience for the investor from that point on.

15.4 Where Do We Go From Here?

If administered, regulated, issued, and traded properly, security tokens promise to revolutionize and democratize investing for all, just as asset-backed securities (ABS) did in the mid-1980s. While ABSs' history has been slightly checkered, it cannot be denied that the ABS market has improved overall market efficiencies in home equity loans, credit card debt, student loans, etc. It did so by pooling and securitizing the cash flows generated from these loans to the larger financial marketplace, which has a much greater capacity to bear and take risks then individual financial institutions would. Hence, the ABS structure is a good thing from the risk-sharing point of view.

Likewise, security tokens could expand the availability of the US$20 trillion alternative investments market in asset classes such as private equity, hedge funds, real estate, infrastructure, and venture capital to a much wider investment audience. Apart from the financial inclusion factor, it would take the retail market's asset allocation strategy to a whole new level.

There are many instances of financial institutions experimenting with blockchain for security issuance and trading. Bond-I is one example of a debt instrument from the World Bank where issuance and trading are recorded using blockchain. Launched in August 2018, bond-i secondary trading in blockchain commenced in May 2019.

Singapore has allowed the issuance of digital securities, too, be they traditional bonds or private equity-backed bonds, and digital token securities for the trading and settlement of the same in smaller denominations. As mentioned previously, there are both Temasek's PE-backed bonds, which was followed by iSTOX issuing tokens on such bonds, and HSBC Singapore and Marketnode's issuance of digital bonds in conjunction with Singtel's corporate bond offering.

15.5 Conclusion

The digitization of financial security issuance, trading, and administration has taken the field of investments to a new era. I expect the more "esoteric" asset classes, once the domain of the rich, private clients, and institutions, especially alternative investments, to be slowly introduced to the retail segment of society as well. As Cherian and Cokeng (2019c) argue, there is no sound reason one can think of as to why ordinary folk should be excluded from what is now considered mainstream finance.

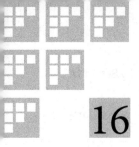

16

The Long March to the Future Economy

Cherian and Lee (2016) pointed out that the Long March was an arduous trek through some of the toughest terrains in China, which allowed Chairman Mao's Red Army to escape Jiangxi after massive losses at the hands of Nationalist forces. It required innovative ways of thinking that allowed Mao's battered forces to regroup and recover.

16.1 Introduction

As the world plans for the future economy — admittedly in a less hazardous environment — we recognize that creativity is key for innovation. At the same time, we must consider the role of government in driving economic initiatives.

While there is no doubt that governments should be sweating the big stuff — driving fundamental research and development, and the necessary regulatory frameworks — a less interventionist approach on the small stuff would probably serve nations well.

We are referring here to the incremental improvements to apps in social media or, in the case of finance, robo-advisors, which provide automated, algorithm-based investment advice.

16.2 When it Comes to Innovation, Laissez-faire is Best

There is increasing evidence that incremental improvements are best left to free enterprise, private capital, and entrepreneurs in true laissez-faire fashion. Market forces should be allowed to prevail to ensure the survival of the fittest and that the economy is more productive in the long run.

In the 1980s, two of the leading technology corridors in the United States were California's Silicon Valley and Massachusetts' Route 128, both located in prime hubs of science and technology education, entrepreneurship, and innovation.

One of them — Route 128 — doesn't exist anymore, while Silicon Valley continues to flourish.

The reasons for this are discussed eloquently by AnnaLee Saxenian in her book, *Regional Advantage: Culture and Competition in Silicon Valley and Route 128*. She argues that Silicon Valley followed the path of encouraging and nurturing individual entrepreneurialism, competition, collaboration, innovation, and informality. On the other hand, Route 128 carried the baggage of mass-production models and hierarchical management structures and adhered to the theory of the firm as only a diehard bureaucrat or micro-economist would.

The true seeds of creativity lie in our younger generation, who require the right educational setting and social environment. The role of government is to ensure every potential "seed" is sown in the right soil to allow it the best chance to germinate and grow creativity.

16.3 No Albatrosses Needed Here

There are several ways to achieve creativity — by providing equal educational experiences for all children where enrichment activities are given within the school and available to all. Society must also adapt to celebrate creativity over conformity, learning over success and failure, and weighing expected costs against expected benefits. In the case of Singapore, it is also possible that the resulting personal asset–liability management needs from a 30-year Housing and Development Board (public leasehold housing) mortgage, while admirable in the context of home ownership at an early stage of one's career and fervently encouraged by the government, could potentially stifle the creative juices of a young entrepreneur.

In the United States, government funding was and still is important in contributing to the development and success of science and technology hubs, spin-off technologies and commercially viable products. Case in point: roughly 86 percent of Massachusetts Institute of Technology's (MIT) total research expenditure of US$1.6 billion in 2015 derived from Federal sources of funding.

Part of the reason is that the nature of capital is different. Government funding tends to be patient and long lived. Its value is as a means to solve major science and technology problems that primarily benefit society, with the potential of a commercializable product at the end of a very long, winding road as a secondary outcome. Private capital, on the other hand, is impatient, given the ultimate objective of private investors to quickly realize a high return on their investment.

Given that one accepts this capital separation, many governments are clearly likely to commit errors based on the belief that they, like Steve Jobs, can predict the future by inventing it.

16.4 On Flexibility, Failure, and Reformation

The key to innovation success is threefold: have the resilience to change; inculcate the mindset to innovate and succeed in a highly disruptive world; and adopt the need to constantly question the status quo. These are almost necessary conditions for truly disruptive jumps and "Eureka" moments to occur, but it is a line of thinking that is often alien to many governments.

A government's positive role is clearly one that provides the necessary ingredients and tools for talent, innovation, and entrepreneurialism to thrive. It is less about leading with policies and prescriptions on innovation. A formulaic and standardized paint-by-numbers DIY kit does not create masterpieces.

One key disruptive force that has the potential to undermine a pillar of any economy is financial technology, or FinTech. According to a recent report, close to US$500 billion (approximately 5 percent) in annual global financial services industry revenues are at risk of disruption by technology-driven firms engaged in FinTech.

PwC's latest Global FinTech Report notes that within the next 5 years, more than 20 percent of financial services business will be at risk from the FinTech industry, with consumer banking and payments the most likely to be disrupted first.

The good news for traditional financial institutions is that only a small fraction of this disruption has actually been realized. Indeed, many financial institutions are now starting their own FinTech initiatives. Many financial institutions have developed digital innovation centres and laboratories, while some also have launched hackathons, incubators, and accelerators to speed up the time-to-market for FinTech products.

Our prediction is that innovation labs of larger or better financial institutions will eventually crowd out or buy out the technology start-ups, along with their designer hoodies and faded jeans, per regulatory and consumer demands, just as some of us would feel more comfortable buying a premium electric car or self-driving vehicle from BMW, Mercedes, or Caltech's Jet Propulsion Lab (recall NASA's fully battery-powered Lunar Roving Vehicle from the early 70s?) over a Tesla or GoogleCar.

16.5 Conclusion

Given the above, it is clear that different segments of society, business, and government will likely need to have different priorities, even as they focus on marching towards the same goal in the future economy. Each segment taking calculated risks and making errors along the way is okay, as long as they are dealt with maturely, just as Professor Michael Frese from the Asia School of Business in Kuala Lumpur suggests, "minimize negative and maximize positive error consequences" (examples of the latter are learning and innovations).

The key is for each to constantly evaluate and challenge the status quo. The dynamic nature of active constructive criticism and/or examination between government, academics, practitioners, and opinion leaders is a hallmark of entrepreneurialism. This is even more important when steering the ship in the current choppy economic waters — even though coordinated on the bridge, each station has an important role to play in successfully reaching our ultimate destination.

Part 3

Macro, Debt, Sustainable, and Political Economy

17

SME Financing: The Need for Out-of-the-Box Thinking for the Next Systemic Crisis*

History has taught us that any pandemic has prodigious human, health, and economic consequences. Even with all the modern advances in health and emergency medical care, the COVID-19 pandemic has taken an extraordinary toll in human lives. As of 1 May 2021, there have been 151 million cases and 3.17 million deaths recorded worldwide. Singapore has at least avoided the worst of the disease's impact; the city-state has witnessed only 61,121 COVID-19 cases and 30 deaths as of 1 May 2021. On the vaccination side, more than 4 percent of the population has received a second dose of the vaccine.

17.1 Impact of COVID-19 on Singapore's SMEs

According to the Ministry of Trade and Industry in Singapore, the country's GDP nonetheless suffered an overall y-o-y contraction of –5.4 percent in 2020, with most of the contraction understandably happening in the second quarter of 2020 (–13.3 percent). Despite estimates that the construction industry will contract by 20.2 percent in the first quarter

---

* This chapter is excerpted from the *Nomura Journal of Asian Capital Markets*, Autumn 2021, Vol. 6, No. 1. See Cherian (2021).

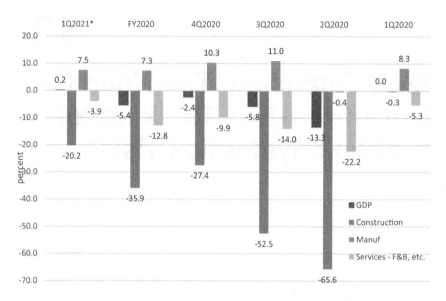

Figure 17.1:   Singapore's gross domestic product in chained (2015) dollars
Note: (1) The GDP estimates for 1Q2021 are computed from data for the first 2 months of the quarter (i.e., January and February 2021) and are subject to revision. (2) Chained dollars are inflation-adjusted real dollar amounts over time that allow the comparison of figures from different years.
Source: Ministry of Trade & Industry (Singapore).

of 2021 (–65.6 percent in 2Q2020), the overall Singapore economy is expected to expand by 0.2 percent on a y-o-y basis in the first quarter of 2021 (Figure 17.1).

The impact on businesses in Singapore, including SMEs and particularly those in the hospitality, travel, tourism, and entertainment sectors, has been more severe. Singapore, like many other responsible governments around the world, came up with massive financial support packages in 2020 and 2021 to help preserve local SMEs, workforce, households, public health and well-being, and the overall economy. Despite the Singapore government's massive COVID financial support, on the order of S$100 billion (US$75 billion) in 2020 (close to 20 percent of GDP) and another planned S$107 billion in Budget 2021, S$53.7 billion (US$40.4 billion) of which will be drawn from its reserves, most government support to business is in the form of loans and debt channelled through the private sector at concessional rates, which eventually have to be repaid.

17.2 Policy Response

In response to COVID-19, the Singapore government helped over 15,300 SMEs improve their productivity, innovation, and internationalization efforts in 2020; this was 54 percent more enterprises than the government assisted in 2019. About S$18 billion in loans at concessionary rates were disbursed. According to the Department of Statistics of Singapore, SMEs are a key pillar of the island-nation's economy. In 2020 (with 2019 data in parenthesis), SMEs contributed 45 percent of value-add to Singapore's GDP of S$480.2 billion (S$507.6 billion), provided over 70 percent of the 3.35 million (3.52 million) in total jobs, and constituted 99.5 percent (99.5 percent) of all its enterprises, comprising 279,700 (273,100) firms. As mentioned, many SMEs in Singapore do not have access to the local capital markets. Instead, they must rely on government support and grants (which are not ample), and bank financing, or are simply owner-financed. Enterprise Singapore's Year-in-Review 2020 provides an overview of the support provided by the government, and the business challenges faced by enterprises (Figure 17.2).

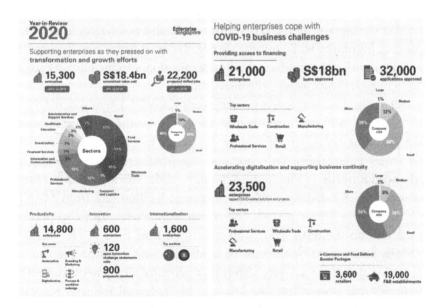

Figure 17.2:   Enterprise Singapore's year-in-review 2020
Source: Enterprise Singapore.

17.3 The Need to do More: The Case for Quasi-equity

As the infographic shows, the need for a long-term solution for all enterprises in Singapore, especially hard-hit SMEs, cannot be overemphasized. Indeed, it is a problem faced the world over. While subsidized or concessionary loans may temporarily help ease firms' short-term burdens, they may end up dragging down businesses in the long run, especially if they are SMEs.

For that reason, I recommend that governments explore the possibility of taking on a partial equity stake in SMEs as part of the overall solution to the "going concern" (or the lack thereof) problem of such firms, both large and small. This approach, only applicable during a large-scale, systemic crisis, should be exercised in the case of SMEs and those firms with limited access to bank loans or capital market fundraising mechanisms. For convenience, I refer to the state's direct equity stake in the business as "quasi-equity" (as opposed to preferred equity or convertible equity). How would a quasi-equity programme work, taking Singapore's experience as an example?

Firstly, the government has to recognize the need to provide support to SMEs during a systemic crisis such as a health pandemic, to keep the economy humming while mitigating negative economic consequences, to save organizational capital, especially organization-specific human capital, and to mitigate negative social consequences.

Secondly, the Singapore government's COVID-19 subsidized term loan scheme, administered by the Monetary Authority of Singapore (MAS) and/or Enterprise Singapore via banks, has greatly helped micro and small enterprises. Very broadly, **the MAS-Enterprise Singapore Enhanced Enterprise Financing Scheme — SME Working Capital Loan** is capped at S\$ 1 million, with a 0.1 percent lending rate from MAS to the banks for a 2-year period. The government shares up to 90 percent of the risk on the SME loan, with the bank's final interest rate charged to SMEs determined by the cost of funds, the SME's risk profile, and so on. It also allows for a 1-year deferral of principal repayment, subject to the bank's risk assessment. The Ministry of Trade and Industry reported that the interest rates ranged between 2 percent and 4.5 percent p.a.,

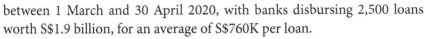

between 1 March and 30 April 2020, with banks disbursing 2,500 loans worth S$1.9 billion, for an average of S$760K per loan.

Thirdly, the government is aware that direct handouts of cash can be costly for the following reasons:

- Handing out money to those who do not need it nor deserve it is costly.
- Fair and justified selective handouts may have high administrative costs, e.g., overcoming firm-specific information asymmetry and moral hazard.

The Singapore government's various enhanced credit channel schemes for SMEs appear to be working well. What is missing? Despite the change in the administration in the U.S., the trend away from globalization towards regionalism pressed by inward-looking policies will continue. Consistent with the (pandemic-related) Declaration on Trade in Essential Goods, and past agreements such as the Closer Economic Partnership (CEP), Strategic Economic Partnership (SEP), and the Free Trade Agreement (FTA), the government announced that SMEs need to "emerge stronger, aspire to be one of the first to recover, seize new business opportunities" post-pandemic.

Regrettably, the world is in transition, with more nationalism and regionalism in evidence. That said, ASEAN nations, particularly Singapore, are seeing more foreign investment coming in to cater to the demands of China, Japan, and the rest of Asia. SMEs in Singapore can be key players in this new phase as the pandemic subsides. However, SMEs with the potential to seize such opportunities in the region and beyond will certainly face financial constraints. Additionally, SMEs will need to redesign, retrain, hire, innovate, upskill, tech-up, and transform. To do this, they will need even more financing — which is the nature of entrepreneurial financing. Banks and traditional financial institutions may be "trapped" with extant SME loans, deferral and forbearance programmes, non-performing or bad loans, etc., so that SMEs are likely to remain cash constrained even after the pandemic fades.

This is where a hybrid entrepreneurial financing solution option, i.e., credit combined with quasi-equity, will be helpful. A quasi-equity overlay example specific to Singapore would be instructive. The textbox below depicts the government's original concessionary lending scheme offered via the banks around March 2020 (Option 1) overlaid with state-funded quasi-equity. For convenience, the government Special Purpose Vehicle (g-SPV) referenced below could potentially be set up under the new Singapore Variable Capital Companies Act (2020).

17.4 Operationalizing State-led Quasi-equity

How does state-led quasi-equity financing work? First, determine which SMEs qualify for the quasi-equity programme via certain quantitative filters, say, the past 3 years' Profits after Tax (PAT), long-term viability/prospects, and the bank's credit loan officers' evaluation, as in Option 1 of the textbox. Then, provide an arms-length, quasi-equity "term financing" via the g-SPV. Say, for example, y percent of 2017–2019 average annual revenues is in equity financing, which is combined with [100-y] percent via the MAS-Enterprise Singapore SME term loan. Like preferred equity, the g-SPV holding the quasi-equity shares has no voting rights but has priority over owners' equity, i.e., the SME pays "dividends" in the form of, say, higher corporate taxes. The SME can buy the quasi-equity back from the g-SPV at an appropriate buy-back or forward price post a fixed holding period or duration. The oversight of the SME as a result of the quasi-equity will involve a Board of Overseers.

Conjoining state-led quasi-equity with the SME enhanced loan scheme provides a first-loss protection mechanism for the lenders. It also has other tangible benefits. On the business front, the SME faces lower interest rates (a reduction of x basis points) and hence lower monthly loan payments. On the lender's front, it fully utilizes the bank's ability to assess loans and lowers risk, given the government's equity participation, ceteris paribus. Additionally, it frees up capital on the bank's balance sheet for other more productive lending. On the government front, it encourages entrepreneurial risk-taking without overclaiming the fruits of the SMEs' efforts (the forward sell-back price is the SMEs' put option). A simple financial economic model is provided in the Appendix to justify the programme economically.

The state-owned g-SPV of the quasi-equity certainly must worry about standard risk management issues, like adverse selection and moral hazard.

For example, due to adverse selection, the SME would know more about its true health, condition, and commitment than the g-SPV does, ex ante. The solution is appreciation for long-term reputational effects, particularly in the case of Singapore, which is a small island-nation. If necessary, the g-SPV can apply an adverse selection "haircut" to the loan/equity financing amount. Another example would be moral hazard, which arises when the SME recipient of quasi-equity financing, ex post, siphons off the funds for unauthorized purposes, be they unnecessary risk-taking or consumption of perquisites. The government, however, has punitive authority: any fraud or egregious wrongdoing can be prosecuted, or the SME could be "blacklisted" by the government.

In a well-managed country like Singapore, where tax compliance is good and long-term reputation is paramount, these effects would be smaller than in many other jurisdictions. Apart from the government agencies and regulatory authorities, reputable local business associations can be incorporated into the Board of Overseers in PPP format to monitor the state-led quasi-equity financing programme.

17.5 Conclusion

In this essay, I have tried to lay out how business owners, investors, and policymakers can use financial markets, products, policies, technology, and science to build more resilient ecosystems to counter extreme systemic crises.

In retirement finance, adequacy and customization are paramount to individual lifecycle planning. Indeed, there are various tools and applications already available to do that in a cost-efficient and seamless manner. Additionally, governments should enact legislation to ring-fence retirement assets from capital invasion.

In SME financing, state-run quasi-equity funding with unique features can help provide the necessary liquidity to an otherwise healthy firm during exigencies. Quasi-equity financing is meant to tide the SME over a difficult (yet short) liquidity "squeeze period" in exchange for equity to help the firm survive, recover, and potentially thrive in the long run.

Appendix: The Mathematics of SME Financing

A simple economic model to illustrate the economic benefit of state-led quasi-equity is instructive[1]:

- There are two states of nature: $q \in \{h, l\}$ [h or high = good state w.p. p; l or low = bad state w.p. $(1 - p)$].
- One SME which can borrow $D \in \{D_L, D_H\}$ at $r = 0$ (i.e., assume borrowing rate = 0%); and $D_L < D_H$.
- SME needs D_H (\$) in total financing, and is risk averse with Von-Neumann Morgenstern utility such that $u'(\cdot) > 0$ and $u'(\cdot) < 0$, where $u(\cdot)$ is the SME's twice continuously differentiable "utility function".
- One good risky investment returning R (in \$) w.p. p and 0 w.p. $(1 - p)$.
- One riskless investment with certain return S (in \$).
- SME can allocate $a \in [0, 1]$ to "good" risky investment and $(1 - a)$ to riskless investment:
  - Scenario 1: All investment financed by debt => $D = D_H$.
  - Scenario 2: Investment financed by combo of debt (D_L) + quasi-equity (E) for x% give-up s.t. $D_L + E = D_H$.
- If $q = h$ (good state),
  - Income y from ME's investment in risky and riskless assets: $yh(a, D) = \{aR + (1 - a)S\} * D_H$.
- If $q = l$ (bad state),
  - Income y from ME's investment in risky and riskless assets: $yl(a, D) = \{(1 - a)S\} * D_H$ (assume $< D_L$).
- The Bank collects: $P \circ \min\{D, y\} = \min\{D, yl\}$ (i.e., it collects full face value in good state w.p. p, and takes over the firm otherwise).
- The Government (x%) collects: $xy = xy^h$ w.p. p (0 otherwise) (i.e., the government receives dividends per its percent equity stake w.p. p).
- SME $(1 - x$%) retains: $(1 - x)y^h - P$ w.p. p (0 otherwise) (i.e., the SME receives residual value after first paying the government and bank its dues w.p. p).

[1] The financial economic model used in this SME Financing section is adapted from "Contract structure, risk sharing, and investment choice", Greg Fisher, *Econometrica*, Vol. 81, No. 3 (2013): 883–939.

The Scenarios:

- **Scenario 1:** $x = 0\%$, $D = D_H$ (Pandemic borrowing situation in Singapore where SMEs are financed by low-interest loans):
  ME maximizes $u(p * \{aR + (1 - a)S\} * D_H - D_H) => u(p * D_H * \{aR + (1 - a)S - 1\})$.
- **Scenario 2:** $x = x\%$, $D = D_L$; where $D_L + E = D_H$ (Proposed hybrid solution for Singapore where SMEs are financed by low-interest loans and state-led quasi-equity):
  ME maximizes $u(p * \{(aR + (1 - a)S) * (1 - x) * D_H - D_L\}) => u(p * D_H * \{(aR + (1 - a)S) * (1 - x) - 1 * (D_L/D_H)\})$.

Scenario 1: Recall, SME maximizes $u(p * D_H * \{aR + (1 - a)S - 1\})$, and
Scenario 2: SME maximizes $u(p * D_H * \{(aR + (1 - a)S) * \underbrace{(1 - x)}_{<1} - 1 * \underbrace{(D_L/D_H)}_{<1}\})$

- By inspection, since $u'(\cdot) > 0 => a_{max}$ (**Scenario 2**) $> a_{max}$ (**Scenario 1**).
- Due to concavity ($u''(\cdot) < 0$), a in both cases are indeed interior maxima.
- Hence, the SME will optimally invest more in the "good" risky investment in Scenario 2.
- From the bank's point of view, the risk of default in Scenario 2 is lower since:
  $$D_L \text{ (Scenario 2)} < D_H \text{ (Scenario 1)}.$$
- From the government's point of view:
  - ❖ Scenario 2 implies more risk taking by SME and, hence, greater economic activity.
  - ❖ The government collects a dividend of: xy^h w.p. $p => x * \{aR + (1 - a)S\} * D_H$ w.p. p.

18

Additional Safeguards for India's Growth Prospects: A Macro-finance Perspective*

18.1 Introduction

The business-friendly results of India's election in 2014 were clearly a mandate for economic growth, offering a renewed opportunity for the world's largest democracy to propel itself into the top league of the world's leading economies.

It augurs well that the initial coordinated framework to drive infrastructure investment and projects is being aggressively put in place by the new government. The recent budget took the first tentative steps in this regard, via the liberalization of foreign direct investment in infrastructure and defence production, though it stopped short of a far-reaching systemic revamp.

This budget is the beginning of a long list of initiatives aimed at rebooting GDP growth.

Looking at what support the financial sector might offer, we suggest here three additional measures and practices that would act as force multipliers to these initiatives and strengthen India's economic revival.

These measures could potentially result in an organic boost to GDP through reduced costs of borrowing for corporate India, as well as for the government, propelling investment and helping to drive further growth.

---

* This chapter is based on the unpublished working paper by Chakravarty and Cherian (June 2014). A gazillion thanks to my long-time co-author and dear friend, Dr. Ranjan Chakravarty, for his excellent contributions to the original article and the current chapter.

18.2 Measure I: Controlling Cost-push Inflation

India's recent spike in inflation has been and continues to be cost-push, driven by galloping domestic food and soaring global energy prices, and exacerbated by chronically deficient supply chain and distribution systems, and an overburdened infrastructure.

The Central Bank, the RBI, has been forced to respond for the past few years by raising interest rates, in contrast to most of the world — clearly a demand-pull measure, and the only policy alternative that it has at its disposal.

Instruments of monetary policy, which consist only of a handful of measures, cannot be expected to be effective in managing this sort of inflation. It is hence unrealistic to expect the Central Bank, as it has done in the past, to exclusively shoulder the burden of inflation management.

In order to support the RBI on the supply side, we suggest the commissioning and execution of an institutional mechanism to aggressively manage resource prices without resorting to price controls.

Even though India itself has commodity exchanges and developed futures and forward markets, as an entity it is routinely exposed to oil, gas, agriculture, and currency spot price volatilities.

A remedy for this is to create a dedicated financial institution for national resource purchasing, operating in a strategic and cost-effective fashion in the derivatives markets.

The principal result would be hedging of commodity and currency prices by producers, suppliers, buyers, and the liquidity providers, with positions managed effectively, in order to keep a tight rein on India's national-level energy and transactional currency exposure.

To facilitate this, an India Special Purpose Vehicle (I-SPV) could be set up. Such a body should be well capitalized and AAA-rated (for funding cost minimization), with an exclusive mandate to conduct consolidated and coordinated global derivatives trading, clearing, and risk management.

Given that the talent and resources for world-class derivatives trading and risk management are readily available in India, this could be accomplished quickly.

Secondly, the main inflationary pressure comes from domestic retail prices of food items. This is significant, as the producer prices of these items have not jumped as much, but rather the issue is with increases systematically occurring further up the supply chain, in spite of all the recent efforts and advancements in agricultural storage and marketization in India.

In the absence of fully exchange-traded valuing of agricultural goods, in the short run physical markets will have to be relied upon, which in turn are supply chain sensitive.

Speeding up the supply chain helps remedy dislocations in supply and demand, which leads to equilibrium pricing. Accordingly, we recommend that discontinuities in the *farm-to-table* supply chain in agricultural products be subjected to ongoing audits in the same vein as used in the financial services industry.

This auditing process, already well established in India's financial services sector, would not only highlight planning deficiencies on an ongoing basis but would also enable the enforcement of project execution, an area that India could well utilize.

18.3 Measure II: Obtaining the Best Financing Rates for the Trillion-dollar Infrastructure Expansion

Infrastructure expansion is where the greatest opportunity and the greatest potential exposure lie.

The government has said that it expects to spend upwards of $1 trillion on infrastructure upgrading between 2014 and 2019, but that figure is simply the aggregate notional value of the projects. The "carry" or interest costs added on to this could be extremely significant.

Additionally, if we were to factor in currency exposure, the resultant risk could be massive. So, what can be done to minimize this exposure?

Infrastructure projects are top-priority national assets. For proper asset creation, simple transfer payments and independent multicurrency loans will prove to be expensive and intractable, especially given the mega projects that are envisaged.

Instead, we suggest that each set of similar infrastructure projects be financed by a proper pool of dedicated loans, bonds, and structures (or liabilities) on the best terms.

This is possible only if the private and public funds flow into another well-capitalized and AAA-rated set of infrastructure I-SPVs. Each entity would then run a number of infrastructure projects, which would be highly related, both on the asset and liability side.

A cost-effective way to execute this would be to engage a portfolio of private equity firms, global reinsurers, sovereign wealth funds, pension plans, and other long-term institutional investors to underwrite these dedicated I-SPVs.

At each stage, financing efficiencies via spread benefits across related I-SPVs would be realized, and material interest cost savings would accrue at the aggregate level.

18.4 Measure III: Controlling India's Sovereign Credit Rating

It is important to note that, with the exception of dedicated and separately rated I-SPVs, all financing costs to India will revert to a spread over India's sovereign credit rating.

It should be borne in mind that a credit rating is a passive grade assigned to a country based on a range of indicators selected by the ratings agencies themselves, such as the current account deficit level, which in turn are driven by other components. In short, a country's credit rating is a macroeconomic assessment by the ratings agencies of a country's ability to repay its debts on time.

In the wake of the Global Financial Crisis, ratings agencies cannot be opaque about their risk assessment methodologies. India, as a consequence, has an opportunity to work with the ratings agencies to minutely understand their scoring approach, and execute the appropriate actions to optimize its own ratings score. We note that discussions have been conducted at both the Ministry of Finance and the RBI previously, and both the recognition of and a knowledge base on this matter already exist at the official level in India. Leveraging on this, a task force should be re-commissioned to actively work on improving India's credit rating.

18.5 Best Practices

Given the pace of expansion that is expected, the most significant parameter that will drive future performance of the Indian economy is the cost of capital.

In this context, priority measures and the roadmaps to achieve them have been suggested above.

These measures would help reduce economic growth risks, yet manage consumer prices better. They could also manage capital costs in the planned massive infrastructure expansion and lower the country risk premium for India, and hence lower the borrowing costs for both the government and India Inc.

In all cases, the talent and commitment needed for the execution of these measures abound in India.

But there are other essential steps to be taken. India must also strive to move up the "Best Places in the World to do Business" rankings.

It currently languishes at 134 — versus China's 16 — in the IFC/World Bank's "Ease of Doing Business" tables.

While the rule of law has to be always upheld and enforced uniformly, it is ironic how on the prosecutorial side, Indian business leaders get hauled before the courts for the smallest infractions. This at the same time as, according to the analysis by India's Association for Democratic Reforms, the country's ministers and lawmakers continuously face criminal, financial, and other prosecutorial actions.

18.6 Conclusion

In addition to the initiatives that are already being put in place by the new government, the above suggested best practices and prudent application of the rule of law could significantly propel the growth and infrastructure components in India's exciting and unfolding development story. The rest of the world, meanwhile, is watching with bated breath.

18.7 Postscript: February 2022 — A Reckoning

It has now been 8 years since the above piece was written. The BJP government has returned to power for a second term in this period. Though these years have been fraught by controversy — mainly on the social front for the BJP government — and massive exogenous shocks to the global supply chains through the Coronavirus pandemic, India's economic performance, on a structural basis, has been surprisingly good, along the parameters outlined above.

We had flagged an improvement in ranking on the World Bank's Ease of Doing Business Report as a key policy objective in the above essay. In 2014, India's rank stood at 136. As of 2021 it had improved to 63. The World Bank has ruled out irregularities in Indian data after an audit of Asian economies, and confirmed the ranking. A number of the suggestions above have been implemented, and though we do not take any credit for their implementation, we are happy to see that the spirit of the above paper is reflected in the Indian government's performance since the paper's writing. There is yet a long way to go. Indeed, a task force dedicated to India breaking into the big leagues along this indicator has been commissioned at the Ministry level.

The other area where we see a strong push is in infrastructure investment. The push on building highways and road networks has been strong. Similarly, clean energy initiatives in wind and power through public–private partnerships have been significant for wealth creation in the private sector. We see the growth of green bonds in India, still in its infancy but bound to pick up. The domestic capital market is not yet fixed income oriented, but once it happens green bonds are bound to become an attractive destination for retail capital.

Another area of great performance is that of the Central Bank. The RBI has evolved from being an interventionist manager of exchange rates and short-end rate shocks to an auction manager with exchange rates and short-term interest rates floating in market-driven bands. This has had a surprisingly strong impact both on exchange rates and interest rates by creating conditions that have decoupled the short end of the Indian yield curve from the US curve, in fact leading to arbitragers favouring the domestic fixed income market.

The area where we see no improvement yet is in the perception of the ratings agencies. The SPV structure we had recommended was to that end. However, that had presupposed a continuing low-rate environment worldwide, which is no longer valid given the onset of inflation in the US. The Brent-INR coupling is also not as fraught with danger in the immediate term as the offshore and onshore Indian commodity spot and forward markets have, over the last 8 years, developed sufficient liquidity in Brent contracts to accommodate price shocks.

In the context of the objectives outlined in the paper above, therefore, the performance from 2014 to date has been robust and augurs well for capital inflows over the next 8 years.

Hazenomics: Facing the Fire

I have also written a few articles not out of subject matter expertise, but merely out of frustration about the lack of action by governments during a natural or man-made disaster. Cherian (2013) and Ang *et al.* (2015) are two related articles regarding the perennial haze problem the countries in Southeast Asia used to face in the past.

19.1 Introduction

Let's suppose you have a chain-smoking neighbour who happens to watch late-night TV with a lit cigarette in hand. You have repeatedly prevailed upon this person not to do so, given the fire risk — but to deaf ears. Sure enough, one night, a huge fire breaks out at his home. It spreads to nearby homes, including yours. What would your reaction be? To just point a finger at the smoker and blame him for not heeding your advice? Or — as soon as you have spotted the blaze — to immediately summon the fire brigade? The choice seems clear: Call the firefighters.

We faced a similar scenario with the June 2013 haze in Southeast Asia, except that it is transboundary in nature, and there is no regional fire brigade to summon. Maybe it is time to have an ASEAN fire brigade.

19.2 Douse the Fire; Ask Questions Later!

Whatever the culpability of the planters, plantations, or governments, the first priority of the day should obviously be to put the fire out and ask questions later. I am not a wildfire or haze expert, but became a back-seat one out of necessity. Just for comparison, it costs the US about S$20M of firefighting equipment, resources, and professionals to fight a 3,000 hectare wildfire. It also takes between 9 to 14 days to put out. The Bengkalis Regency blaze in Sumatra's Riau province, which caused the haze in Singapore and Malaysia, is about 3,000 hectares. The US experience also involves thousands of support professionals (such as smokejumpers and firefighters), sensor-equipped early-warning aircraft directing the aerial and ground-based firefighting efforts, and air tankers ranging in size that can unleash a deluge of water and fire retardants. These firefighting air tankers include larger 78,000 litre 747 and DC-10 "super heavies", medium-sized Bombardier 415 "superscoopers" with a 6,140 litre capacity, or much smaller scooper helicopters.

If ASEAN doesn't have these critically needed assets to fight our perennial wildfires, its three most affected members should start acquiring them. If costs are a concern, instead of an outright purchase, perhaps leasing options from countries such as the US may be explored. The training, staffing, and maintenance of the brigade would be shared by the multiple agencies involved in fighting fires in these countries. Assistance could also be provided by wealthy donor countries and organizations interested in protecting the environment. It must be noted that any tri-country firefighting exercise will need both Singapore's and Malaysia's resources and support, along with Indonesia's consent; the good news is that this has been done before. Operation Haze in September 1997 was the biggest cross-border firefighting mission in history. It involved teams of Malaysian and Indonesian firefighters battling haze-causing fires in Sumatra and Kalimantan. It was viewed as a cross-border cooperation and coordination event of such importance that the History Channel made a television documentary about it.

There have also been numerous good suggestions made by various experts. Apart from the aforementioned firefighting equipment and fire brigade, it would take a combination of enforceable legislation, economic cost/benefit trade-off analysis, whistle-blower schemes, boycotts, and goodwill. Let us view these in some detail.

19.3 Extraterritorial Legislation

As NUS Professor Ivan Png pointed out in an October 2012 *Straits Times* opinion article and Professor Tommy Koh in a more recent one in the same paper, international law has provisions for transboundary environmental and criminal liability. Indeed, it may only require minor amendments to extant Singaporean and Malaysian environmental laws to pursue extraterritorial legislative reach. One issue here is legislative reach in relation to foreign plantation owners — a case of "practising what we preach at home first". For that, we can always turn to the Grand Master of extraterritorial taxation and legislation for ideas: the US has the Foreign Corrupt Practices Act (FCPA). The FCPA applies to any US business, national, citizen, or resident acting in furtherance of a corrupt practice in a foreign country **whether or not they are physically present in the United States**. Malaysia and Singapore could similarly legislate to prosecute their plantation owners who, say, commit arson in Riau.

If we are really bold, we can go a step further. They might even want to take a cue from extant EU-wide legislation, by mooting a common set of ASEAN laws and regulations that address our common interests, which certainly include the environment and general well-being. Violators could be referred to an EU-style **ASEAN Court of Justice**. Lastly, a whistle-blower programme with an attached reward and "witness protection" scheme, as Prof. Png points out, might see plantation employees prepared to "spill the beans" without fear of reprisals from their bosses.

19.4 Economics — Cost/Benefit Analysis

Professor Euston Quah in a *Straits Times* opinion article written on 24 June 2013 encouraged ASEAN to apply dollars and sense to the haze situation. Singapore is now a S$1 billion per working day economy, of which tourism is about 4 percent (S$40 million). If tourism alone sees a haze "haircut" of 10 percent, that's S$4 million per day.[1] As stated, it

---

[1] "By the numbers: Economic impact of Southeast Asia's haze" (Al Jazeera, 13 Sept 2019). URL: https://www.aljazeera.com/ajimpact/numbers-economic-impact-southeast-asia-haze-190913071603650.html.

will cost approximately S$20M of able tri-country aerial firefighting and ground support to fight the 3,000 hectares of wildfires in Riau. This cost translates roughly to S$6,700 per hectare. (On the other hand, it just takes a few dollars per hectare to start a plantation fire.)

To put this in economic cost/benefit trade-off terms, the firefighting cost has a payback of about 5 days based on Singapore's tourism receipts alone. But wouldn't it be even better if plantation owners clear forests the non-incendiary way in the first place, as Professor Helena Varrkey of University of Malaya in Malaysia has pointed out? She has been publishing research papers on the ASEAN transboundary haze problem since 2008. According to her research, using machines to clear the land would cost plantation owners about S$240 per hectare.

19.5 Collective Responsibility

Taking a leaf from the successful experience of the oil industry, Mr. Kyle Lee, a retired partner of PricewaterhouseCoopers, has suggested the formation of a plantation equivalent to the Oil Spill Response Limited (OSRL) agency, whose responsibility it would be to respond effectively to wildfires on plantation land wherever they may occur. This way, the various regional government agencies and industry players, such as this plantation-owned firefighting cooperative, could form a transboundary force to fight plantation fires. Professor Varrkey argues that most commercial plantations, despite their denials, prefer to use fire ("slash and burn") for cost-related reasons. They are just better at avoiding apprehension. A mandated industry-owned cooperative to fight plantation fires is hence highly warranted. The three governments will need to join hands to ensure this outcome. Since the ASEAN Secretariat's stated mission is to "initiate, facilitate and coordinate ASEAN stakeholder collaboration", it is the natural choice for commanding the brigade.

While the brigade can have its assets placed in various countries, Singapore, with its superior technology in the air and on the ground, advantageous location, and lack of forest fires, would be a natural site for the brigade's headquarters. On a positive note, the Malaysian Maritime Enforcement Agency already has two Bombardier 415 "superscooper" aircraft; their service was recently offered to Indonesia, along with firefighting personnel.

19.6 Conclusion

Arising from these expert opinions and information, it is clear that — to address the raze and haze problem — we need to disabuse ourselves of the belief that garden hoses, cloud-seeding, and a couple of light scooper helicopters with buckets can fight the fires of the magnitude we have seen. The acquisition or leasing of firefighting air tankers, coupled with the efficient deployment of extensive material and human firefighting assets, comprehensive and enforceable legislation, close regional diplomatic cooperation, appropriate financial incentives, political will, and finally, common sense, will help the region get through this and future fires. The outlook isn't hazy.

20

The State As Insurer of Last Resort*

20.1 Introduction — Finance 101

Arrow-Debreu (A-D) securities, which were postulated in the 1950s, demonstrate how in complete markets any payoff structure can be obtained by a linear combination of the underlying "pure" A-D securities. Put simply, state-contingent contracts with arbitrary payoff structures could be constructed to allow investors to hedge or insure against any undesirable outcome, state of nature, and/or aggregate risk.

In some cases, systematic risks can be insured or hedged against, for example, by using put options (futures) on the S&P 500 to insure (hedge) against market declines, or catastrophic bonds in the event of natural disasters.

In other cases — either due to market breakdowns or the inability of the market to bear all the associated risks from a cost, institutional, or regulatory perspective — this is not possible. Say, in the case of inflation or pandemic disease risk. In such circumstances, the state has a distinctive role to play as the insurer of last resort.

The world is now facing a pandemic of catastrophic health and economic consequences globally. To break the chain of the coronavirus transmission and mitigate the attendant public health threat — commonly known as "flattening the contagion curve" (most akin to a Central Bank's

---

*This chapter is excerpted from *Impact of COVID-19 on Asian Economies and Policy Responses*, World Scientific, January 2021.

yield curve flattening exercise by pursuing unconventional monetary policy) — almost all countries are imposing lockdowns to reduce human mobility and face-to-face interactions. Yet, many economic activities rely on just that.

The vigilant measures generate a huge negative supply and demand shock, and disrupt global production value chains and trade greatly. The consequence is a significant decline in output, surge in unemployment, bankruptcy, and worries over financial stability. Many have remarked that the current economic setback is more serious than the Global Financial Crisis the world experienced in 2008–09, while a few have postulated it could be as bad as the Great Depression of the 1930s.

As we know from the economic trade-off literature, there is also no free lunch in business and finance. Every action taken by governments to stem the virus's spread has an economic cost. Some economic sectors have effectively shut down during this pandemic, taking a toll on incomes, jobs, growth, and even inter-nation goodwill and policy coordination. The policy question is how we sustain the economy *ad interim* so that it can recover and thrive when the virus pandemic is behind us.

A financial market analogue would be useful. During periods of extreme stress, Treasury markets have been known to go helter-skelter in prices, for example, when there's a technical squeeze on a particular Treasury bond. This will result in its price rising to an abnormally high level temporarily. Let's assume investor A was massively short of the bond prior to the squeeze occurring. Margin calls during the temporary elevation in price could overwhelm the liquidity condition or solvency of A in the *short run*, even though A's short position could have been the right call in the *long run*. In the extreme case, it could lead to A's bankruptcy.

However, if a deep-pocketed government fund comes to A's rescue by providing the necessary liquidity to tide A over the difficult (yet short run) "squeeze period" in exchange for equity, or the government reopens that particular Treasury issue to alleviate the squeeze, investor A could survive, recover, and potentially thrive in the long run. In other words, when markets break down, be it due to a technical squeeze on Treasuries, a terrorist attack, or a global pandemic, and there isn't any way to hedge against it using the equivalent of A-D securities, the government must step in and provide the necessary relief.

20.2 The Point

Thus, there is theoretical justification for the state to undertake responsibility to insure its members against exogenous systemic negative shocks. Rescue plans are plentiful, and Singapore's plans have the hallmarks of most rescue plans. We use Singapore's rescue plans to date, which amounts to about 12 percent of its gross domestic product, to illustrate. In addition to bolstering the resources available to the healthcare system given this is a pandemic, Singapore's include these essential features:

a. addressing individuals' immediate hardships and covering their basic needs;

b. mitigating job market disruptions and preventing permanent damage to businesses' organizational capital, particularly those in the hard-hit industries like transportation, tourism, retail, and restaurants;

c. maintaining market-wide financial stability and individual financial security, mostly via forbearance programmes, interest and principal payment deferrals, and contractual obligation temporary relief.

20.3 Cash and Hurry!

First, there was the express delivery of cash into Singaporeans' accounts starting in mid-April 2020, with more help given to the lower income. Why targeted cash handouts? A carefully calibrated and targeted cash scheme would be advantageous for both the individuals and the economy. Research shows students, lower-income households, and retirees on fixed incomes spend cash gifts more quickly. This is because they need cash the most, especially during a sudden exigency, and hence spend it the fastest. Additionally, the expeditious manner of their spending helps stabilize the economy the quickest. This double-happiness effect stems from such a policy.

To this point, the Singapore government in its recent Budget 2020, introduced a series of carefully targeted cash payouts, workfare special payments, grocery and sales vouchers, and rebates on service and conservancy charges (a form of homeowners' association fee), particularly for the lower-income households and self-employed.

20.4 Flatteners, Forbearance, and Force Majeure

Second, as part of the COVID-19 financial support programme for individuals and households, various governments also offered mortgage and interest payment relief through the suspension of mortgage payments itself or refinancing opportunities from interest rate cuts and tax holidays.

In Singapore, the central bank announced that qualifying individuals can apply to defer both principal and interest repayment of residential property loans, while small and medium-sized enterprises (SMEs) can defer principal payments on secured term loans up until year end. They can also apply to defer payments on health and life insurance programmes for up to 6 months, and tax payments by 3 months.

The Singapore Ministry of Law is also proposing a law that provides "temporary relief from legal action — on a just and equitable basis — to individuals and businesses who are unable to fulfil their contractual obligations due to COVID-19." This relief would be for a period of up to 6 months and extendable for another six. Such a state-led measure of the first order dominates a scenario where companies independently declare *force majeure* during this pandemic period.

Any extra spending money in an individual's pocket from the package is not going to be a game-changer for household savings and investments. It's meant more to tide people over this difficult and turbulent period. That said, having various private and state-provisioned "insurance" policies, be it for health, unemployment, disability, death, stock market crashes, or pandemics, is always important, in both normal and turbulent times.

20.5 Save the Post and Organizational Capital

Third, saving jobs is important. As a quick-thinking *New York Times* editorial pointed out on 26 March 2020, *Preserving jobs is important because a job isn't merely about the money. Compensated labor provides a sense of independence, identity and purpose; an unemployment check does not replace any of those things. Additionally, a substantial body of research on earlier economic downturns documents that people who lose jobs, even if they eventually find new ones, suffer lasting damage to their earnings potential, health and even the prospects of their children.*

Singapore has indeed stepped up to the plate on the employment front by asking employers not to resort to layoffs and no-pay leaves. To motivate employers in that direction, the government pays out 75 percent of all local employees' wages for the local lockdown month of April, with 25 percent coverage for another 8 months after that, with much higher subsidies — up to 75 percent — for the sectors most affected by this pandemic. This includes employers' contributions to the mandatory social security savings scheme.

This programme, essentially a temporary subsidy, incentivizes companies not to break up their human capital or work teams, and possibly cleverly deploy them for other meaningful activities such as problem-solving the company's operational stresses due to lockdown measures.

Stabilization and support extend beyond mitigating job losses. It includes economy-wide measures to help businesses survive the undue pressures on cash flows arising from an exogenous systemic shock; this is like insuring investment on building organizational capital. Singapore's package offers property tax and corporate income tax rebates, waiver of government rental charges, and bridge loans to cover short-term cash shortfalls.

20.6 Respect and Tech for Elders

Fourth, the impact of the pandemic is particularly severe on senior care and retirees' savings.

Asia in general and Singapore in particular face an ageing population. The death rate of the infected is disproportionately high for seniors. Note, however, eldercare, housing, nursing homes, and retirement facilities have been gaining popularity in ageing Asia regions. The deadly experience of the Seattle-area nursing homes to COVID-19 may change the rules for eldercare.

To mitigate the risk of exposing the elderly to COVID-19, serving them requires less reliance on human mobility, where caregivers, entertainers, volunteers, and healthcare workers deploy in multiple locations. Instead, there should be more dependence on dedicated teams, technology, and faster response times during crises. The Singapore government suspended seniors' social activities, and encourages institutions involved in eldercare to replace physical visits with technologies such as teleconferencing via smartphones to both help them become digitally savvy and to lead more independent and empowered lives.

The trend has to be sustained. Transforming elderly care habits, systems, and infrastructure to the new world order requires asset owners' patient capital and participation. Pension plans and sovereign funds with socially responsible investment motivations may be the natural long-term capital provider or partner for this transformation.

Last but not least, the pandemic-induced global economic stress greatly erodes the principal and earnings of seniors' savings. The Singapore government took bold steps to raise the "silver support" (support to the retired) by 20 percent.

20.7 Post-pandemonium Coordination

Financial economics is an applied science that deals with the intertemporal allocation of scarce resources under conditions of uncertainty and unexpected shocks. While a well-endowed state can come to the rescue when financial markets and products cannot, it could also cause serious problems if central banks and government funds are all rushing for the door at the same time, raising funds to finance their massive stimulus packages. It would be a fire sale of the most liquid — and probably most highly correlated — assets of unimaginable proportions.

20.8 Conclusion

This brings us to our concluding thoughts. Since the COVID-19 disease is a global problem, some form of multilateral policy coordination is necessary for humanity to succeed in curing us of this pandemic as well as for economies to recover. While there are reports of the IMF providing credit lines for poorer nations, or a few central banks arranging for bilateral currency swap lines to ease the virus-related strains on credit markets and provide US dollar liquidity to financial institutions, there is an urgent call-to-action for right-minded political leaders to do much more — systematically and on the global coordination front. At this juncture, it is paramount that the two most powerful nations on this earth join hands to promote international cooperation, a wish we harbour for humanity's sake. Unfortunately, the opposite is happening, which will aggravate the world's suffering.

On the bright side, every global crisis presents opportunities for our collective learning, to alleviate suffering amongst the lower-income groups and SMEs, and to generally improve financial economic outcomes while maximizing social welfare.

21

Financial Trade-Offs Matter during Pandemics*

21.1 Introduction

Forecasts of the trajectory of a pandemic's spread, its effects, and outcomes, be it in the total number of cases, daily new cases, attendant growth rates, recovered and discharged, serious and critical, and, finally, the number of deaths, are critical data for policymakers, public health authorities and healthcare professionals. This is for them to prepare appropriately for the pandemic, allocate medical resources and equipment efficiently, and make optimal life and death decisions (where necessary) in an informed manner.

Likewise, financial markets and the global economy are not immune to a virus's pandemic effect. Governments, central banks, traders, asset managers, pension and sovereign funds, and individuals also react to the trajectory taken by the virus pandemic in terms of total cases, recovery, and death statistics, spread, non-pharmaceutical mitigation or suppression, and movement control (or lockdowns). Current and prospective demand and supply curves are affected, as reflected in stock and bond prices, resulting in financial market turmoil and the attendant downward "self-fulfilling spirals" that come with it, be it in prices, credit, or liquidity.

Finance 101 informs us that there is no free lunch in business and finance. Every prevention action taken by governments to stem the virus's spread — however necessary to "flatten the curve" — has an economic cost. Some economic sectors have effectively shut down during this pandemic,

---

* This chapter is excerpted from *Asia Asset Management*, 14 April 2020. See Cherian (2020).

taking a toll on incomes, jobs, growth, supply chains, and inter-nation goodwill. Unsurprisingly, one economist's private forecast of 1Q2020's year-on-year growth in China is as low as –6.5 percent, which is around the estimated impact of 2Q2003's year-on-year growth in China from the SARS outbreak of 2003. Sell-side economists now expect "a global recession in 2020 of similar magnitude to the recessions of 1982 and 2009", with predictions for 2020 global GDP growth as low as –2.0 percent, a far cry from Goldman Sachs' economics research team's +3.4 percent forecast in November 2019. In early March, the OECD had revised the expected economic growth for all countries downwards, as shown in Figure 21.1.

We address three issues here. How the current lockdown does the following:

1. provides meaningful learnings, both positive and negative, particularly the learnings from policymaking in Asia in response to the COVID-19 pandemic,
2. impacts individuals in their savings and investing behaviour, and
3. opens new opportunities for financial economics research, particularly for Asia.

What is the efficacy of these programmes and did any country do it better than the rest?

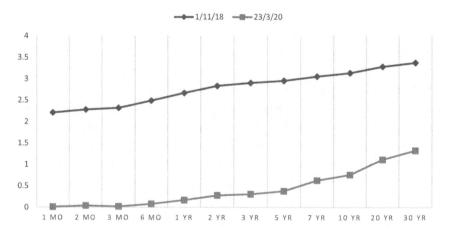

Figure 21.1:   Treasury yields (23 March 2020 versus November 2018)
Source: Interest Rate Statistics, US Department of Treasury.

21.2 Cash is King

All forms of help to household finances in times of extreme balance sheet stress is certainly a good thing overall. Case in point, the high point of the US financial support programme, based on a White House idea, was to mail US$1,200 checks to all adults within American households who earn US$75,000 or less, with an additional US$500 for each child in that household. Hong Kong handed out a flat amount of HK10,000 (US$1,290) in cash to every adult permanent resident as part of its scheme.

That said, such transfers and support should be targeted. A carefully calibrated scheme would be more beneficial for both individuals and the economy. Academic research has shown that students, lower-income households, retired elderly on fixed incomes, etc., spend cash gifts more quickly. This is because they need it the most, especially during a sudden exigency, hence spend it the fastest. Additionally, the expeditious manner of their spending also helps stimulate the economy the quickest. The result? A *double-happiness* effect that stems from a targeted cash handout policy. To this point, the Singapore government recently introduced a series of carefully devised and targeted vouchers, cash payment schemes, and rebates in its *Care and Support Package*, particularly for lower-income households within Singapore's Budget 2020.

21.3 Home on the (Mortgage) Range

On the home mortgage side, with homeownership rates in the US and Canada averaging around 65 percent, Singapore around 90 percent, and Italy around 73 percent, recent measures, such as the UK and US cutting interest rates, Italy and UK pledging to suspend mortgage payments, as well as Canadian banks and the US government calling for 6 to 12 months of mortgage forbearance, are all good for the consumer's wallet. Malaysia and Singapore also introduced loan deferral, moratorium and restructuring programmes, as well as reduced financing costs for households, corporates, and SMEs. Due to lower interest rates, there's massive mortgage refinancing taking place right now in the US, and potentially in the UK. For example, in November 2018, the 30-year fixed rate mortgage in the US was around 4.9 percent. It is around 3.3 percent now, which is an all-time low within

50 years, while the 15-year fixed rate is around 2.8 percent. Treasury yields, as indicated in Figure 21.1, explain why that is the case.

Again, lower interest rates imply more money in consumers' pockets for spending purposes, be it for nutrition, healthcare, or exigencies. However, on the flip side, the holders of these mortgage loans, mortgage-based bonds, and securities are taking a hit with the prepayments, suspensions, and forbearance. That counterparty angst must be prudently addressed as well.

It is worth noting that the above extra spending money is not going to be a game-changer for household savings and investments. It's meant more to tide people over this difficult and turbulent period.

21.4 Informed Modern Portfolio Theory

From the investments perspective, for those who have been heavily invested in stocks and lost a lot of money, it may be the worst time to panic and get out of those investments. Additionally, households should take a long-term "total portfolio management" approach, i.e., your job (viz. monthly income), your house (viz. a form of store of value), your financial investments, and insurance policies are all part of the total portfolio management approach. Only act if you are not well diversified in the total portfolio perspective for the long haul. In summary, you may not need to do anything now as you may already be well-diversified, hedged, and insured!

In order to insure against bad outcomes, having various insurance policies, be it for health, unemployment, disability, death, stock market crashes, or viruses is always important in turbulent times. This is perhaps a lesson to remember for a future crisis.

A reasonable question is how far ahead individuals should be planning for this crisis and what should the minimum financial cushion be. Part of that answer lies in how long COVID-19 will last. In this pandemic, we have a containment problem: asymptomatic patients could silently spread the virus via "stealth transmission." This makes effective containment an issue unless the authorities impose a total lockdown, such as the one imposed on Hubei Province. So, we can just hope for the best and be tactical.

Financial markets may have their own views on the duration of the pandemic. A *back-of-the-envelope* calculation of S&P 500 Implied

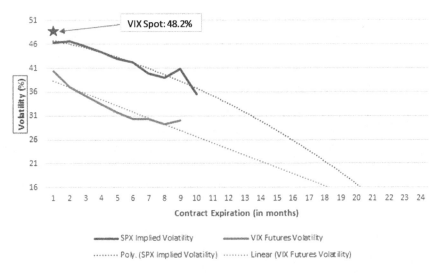

Figure 21.2:   Term structure of S&P 500 implied volatilities versus VIX futures volatilities
Source: CBOE.

Volatilities and VIX Futures Volatilities may perhaps give some indication of the market's view of how long this pandemic will last. Since S&P 500 market volatility is historically around 16 percent, it appears by extrapolation that financial markets (in a forward-looking sense) forecast that markets won't stabilize for at least another 18 months (see volatility curves' *x*-axis crossing points in Figure 21.2). Apart from that extrapolation, the volatility curves also appear to be in "backwardation". This implies that spot volatility is higher than futures and implied volatilities, which is a rare occurrence for S&P 500 volatility curves. Backwardation simply indicates that there's a lot of uncertainty on uncertainty here!

In any case, given cash is always king in any crisis, ensuring you have enough of it stashed away for acquiring baseline health, nutrition, and emergency care for up to 18 months isn't unwise.

21.5 The Ageing Process Ripe for Disruption?

Asia also faces an ageing population. As a result, elderly care, housing, nursing homes, and retirement facilities have been gaining popularity in this region. However, the deadly experience of the Seattle-area nursing homes during COVID-19 may change the rules for elderly care. There will likely be less reliance on human mobility — where caregivers, entertainers, volunteers, and healthcare workers work in multiple locations, a factor which contributed to the rapid spread of the virus amongst the elderly in Seattle. Instead, there will potentially be more dependence on dedicated teams, technology (social distancing, FaceTime, online entertainment and games, telemedicine, etc.), and faster response times during crisis situations.

Indeed, one of the earliest coronavirus-related suspensions carried out in Singapore was on seniors' social activities, which are commonplace during non-pandemic times. The government and institutions involved in elderly care simultaneously encouraged caregivers to replace physical visits with "new technologies for the elderly, like teleconferencing using smartphones and WiFi, in order to help them be digitally-savvy and lead a more independent and empowered life."

Transforming elderly care habits, systems, and infrastructure to the new world order may require asset owners' patient capital and participation. Herein, pension plans and sovereign funds with ESG motivations may be the natural long-term capital provider or partner for this transformation in elderly care.

21.6 Additional Opportunities for Research

Financial economics is an applied science that deals with the intertemporal allocation of scarce resources under conditions of uncertainty and unexpected shocks. On the bright side, every crisis presents finance research opportunities for our collective learning, to alleviate suffering amongst the lower income, and to generally improve the individual's financial economic outcomes while maximizing social welfare in a Pareto-efficient manner.

The main research opportunity that comes to mind is *Nudge Economics*. How can policymakers quickly offer highly targeted economic incentives and behavioural nudges to encourage the public to do the right thing during a pandemic or extreme crisis event, be it in finance, spending, or social behaviours?

Also up for consideration are steps that can be taken by retailers, the online marketplace, health providers, and presently strained segments of the economy to support the reasonable distribution of seemingly scarce resources whilst minimizing contagion potential. With irrational behaviour, such as hand sanitizer or toilet paper hoarding, adequate incentive-based measures and good communications by the relevant authorities are crucial. An evidence-based collation and discussion of the efficacy of recent measures, such as that of dedicated elderly shopping hours, communication from governments on available stockpiles, limits on the number of items purchased per customer, and innovative pricing to prevent goods hoarding, would lend empirical perspective to what has and has not worked.

Another issue that remains to be researched is operationalizing the long-term total portfolio management concept for household consumption and investment decision-making. This not only involves functions such as borrowing, saving, and investing but also hedging and insurance.

21.7 Conclusion

Akin to Robert Merton's seminal research on lifetime consumption and optimal portfolio rules from the early 70s, which yielded both a CAPM-type diversification portfolio and multiple "factor hedging" portfolios as naturally arising occurrences from an individual facing multiple dimensions of uncertainty when making intertemporal financial decisions, the introduction of labour income, retirement planning, housing values, event risk, unexpected shocks, etc., could also yield different approaches to extant personal financial advice, intermediation, products, market structures, and regulations.

In the meantime, our parting remark to individuals would be to skip the luxuries for later, when our health and economies recover, and focus on the necessities for now, like eating and staying healthy.

22

A Turning Point Moment of Interest (or Why Is Everyone Afraid of Inflation?)*

22.1 Introduction

At every turning point in financial markets' history, lessons are learned, predictions and strategies updated, and regulations put in place to mitigate the crisis that was. Charles Kindleberger, in his 1978 book *Manias, Panics & Crashes*, depicted it well: There are historical regularities in all past major crises. These turning points — particularly when not anticipated and priced in by the market — are not only potential triggers of crisis but also offer great opportunities for asset managers who are appropriately prepared.

22.2 After Decades of Declines, Inflation and Interest Rates May be on the Uptrend

Two fundamental variables that have not had a structural turning point for decades are interest rates and inflation. Both have been on the decline in major economies since the early 1980. In the US, the consumer price index peaked at 14.6 percent in April 1980 and the benchmark 10-year government bond yield hit a high of 15.5 percent in September 1981 (Figure 22.1).

---

* This chapter is excerpted from *Asia Asset Management,* 25th Anniversary Special Edition Issue, November–December 2021. See Cherian and Khatri (2021).

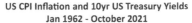

Source: FRED, Federal Reserve Bank of St. Louis; https://fred.stlouisfed.org/series/CPIAUCSL, November 14, 2021.

Figure 22.1:   US CPI and 10-year treasury yields

Most recently, the 10-year Treasury bond has been yielding 1.56 percent (November 12, 2021), down from a peak of 1.74 percent on March 31 after a pandemic-related low of around 0.5 percent — and an all-time intra-day trough of 0.318 percent — in March 2020. The 10-year US Treasury Inflation-Protected Security (TIPS) was trading even "richer" on November 12, at a yield of minus 1.16 percent.

22.3 What Gives?

There appear to be heightened concerns lately over the US benchmark interest rate taking a turn for the worse. This rate rise fear was compounded by multi-decade highs in inflation and the Federal Reserve starting to taper its bond purchases, as well as other demand and supply factors, such as the reduced allocation by the Japanese pension giant, Government Pension Investment Fund, to US government bonds.

Quantitative easing, or QE, which was deployed in the wake of the 2008 global financial crisis, is designed to support economic activity beyond the lower bound of policy interest rates. Tapering refers to trimming bond purchases, which is effectively reducing the support provided by monetary policy. The turning point in monetary policy signalled by tapering has been disruptive in recent years, as highlighted by the "taper tantrum" in 2013, particularly in emerging markets.

Inflation has also begun rising at a fairly fast clip in the US. The headline consumer price index rose 6.2 percent year on year in October. While recent readings have been unexpectedly high, this is also partly due to base effects — demand and prices were both muted when the US economy was in the throes of the coronavirus crisis last year — and supply chain disruptions.

Market reaction during the rise in yields was to quickly rotate out of interest rate-sensitive stocks and sectors towards those that fare well in a robust and growing economy. Although yields have since retreated slightly, pulled back up, and now are fairly range bound, market sentiment and fears remain persistent for now.

22.4 Issues for Asset Managers

For asset managers and owners, there are two related issues as far as longer-term bond yields are concerned. The first is, what determines longer-term interest rates? And secondly, what drove the secular decline in short- and long-term interest rates since the 1980s to their current historic lows, which includes negative rates in some developed markets?

To understand the first, it's helpful to decompose long-term interest rates, such as the 10-year US Treasury yield, into three components: expected inflation, expectations about the future path of real short-term interest rates, and the term premium.

Former Fed Chairman Ben Bernanke, in a blog post published on the website of the Brookings Institution, attributes changes in the term premium to changes in both the perceived riskiness of the long-term security and demand/supply factors. We might add that this riskiness element of the term premium can be further broken down into the uncertainty about the inflation outlook and the real rate outlook associated with uncertainty about the economic recovery.

We think demand and supply factors in bond markets also deserve special attention. This is in the context of changes in capital reserve requirements, technological disruptions, be it financial technology — and

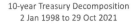

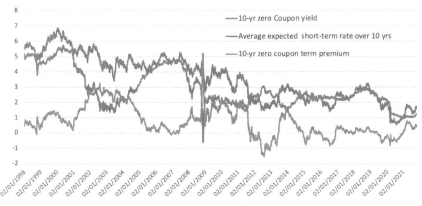

Source: https://www.frbsf.org/economic-research/indicators-data/treasury-yield-premiums/ ; accessed 21 November

Figure 22.2:   US 10-year treasury decomposition

particularly crypto assets — structural and institutional factors in repo markets, or macro shocks.

When decomposing long-term yields from their peak in 1981 to the current lows, all three elements pointed out by Bernanke have contributed to the secular decline (Figure 22.2).

22.5 Why did Inflation Expectations Decline?

US inflation expectations declined sharply by the mid-1980s from their peak in 1980. This is often attributed to factors such as Paul Volker's aggressive hiking of policy rates — and the associated recession — which credibly brought down inflation and inflation expectations, and the Nobel Prize-winning insights of Finn Kydland and Edward Prescott about the time inconsistency problem in policy. These insights emphasized the benefits of rules, inflation-targeting frameworks, and careful communications in building monetary policy credibility.

Another important factor for most major economies was the reduction in post-War debt to gross domestic product ratio by the late 1970s, which allowed the monetary policy to focus more on inflation than on debt servicing costs — in other words, a shift away from fiscal dominance.

22.6 Why Did Rates Decline?

It is real, or inflation-adjusted, interest rates that matter for an economy, particularly via investment and savings decisions. Recall the concept of the natural rate of interest, or r^*, which is the real rate consistent with an economy at full employment and stable inflation, i.e., around the desired target rate.

While central banks can control nominal short-term policy rates, r^* is ultimately driven by economic forces in free markets, and is typically related to potential growth and fiscal policy. The decline in r^* across major economies, as estimated by the Fed (Figure 22.3), is in the context of declining potential growth estimates. Importantly, real rates have continued to decline despite the rapid buildup in government debt in major economies, particularly since 2008.

A recent paper by the European Union's European Systemic Risk Board (ESRB) summarizes nicely the likely long-term drivers of the decline. Their "structural view" considers factors driving the savings–investment gap, including demographics, i.e., increasing life expectancy and slowing

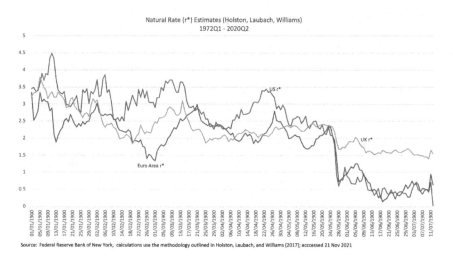

Figure 22.3:   Natural rate (r^*) estimates for US, Euro Area, and UK

population growth driving savings, the relative decline in the price of investment goods, and rising inequality.

The "financial cycle view" of why rates are low highlights factors such as financial deregulation, excessive monetary expansion, misplaced optimism about economic prospects, and the "balance sheet recession" in the wake of the global financial crisis.

The ESRB paper also cites a number of other papers, which look over a long span of history at past pandemics and natural disasters. These works suggest the COVID-19 pandemic can have a downward impact on interest rates for a prolonged period ahead.

22.7 Term Premiums

Term premium, as previously stated, represents risks and uncertainty about the inflation outlook and the real interest rate outlook. The factors discussed above have, since the early 1980s, resulted in more anchored inflation expectations and thus less risk stemming from the inflation outlook. In the post-global financial crisis period, unconventional monetary policies, including QE, the long duration of assets purchased, and forward guidance, serve to reduce uncertainty around short-term policy rates and contribute to compression in the term premium. The recent market sentiment about monetary policy normalization and inflation are consistent with the moves in the estimated term premium this year (Figure 22.2).

22.8 Inflection Point?

In the near to medium term, as the US and other major economies achieve high levels of vaccinations, recoveries are expected to progress, and output gaps are expected to close. Interest rate futures are now pricing in at least two Fed rate hikes in 2022.

Indeed, some emerging markets are already raising policy rates. Prospects for the continued secular decline in nominal interest rates depend on two things: the underlying factors continuing and how near we are to the effective lower bound (ELB).

Economists once considered zero to be the lower bound for policy rates, but the post-global financial crisis experience demonstrates that policy rates can go into negative territory. Even then, there is still a limit to how negative nominal rates can go given the various alternatives to holding cash. If the factors described above continue to push r^* down, nominal rates will eventually hit the ELB and hence reach an inflection point after four decades of secular declines. Further reductions in r^* can of course still be achieved through higher inflation.

Like interest rates, inflation might be hitting cyclical and secular turning points. We consider the following prospective drivers of turning points in inflation: a monetary view of inflation (inflation is ultimately driven by excess money growth in the long run); an excess demand view of inflation (the short-term Phillips Curve with inflation within a cycle being related to the output gap); supply-side factors (including trade, supply chains, and climate change-related issues); and fiscal drivers of inflation.

22.8.1 Money growth and inflation

Milton Friedman famously stated that "inflation is always and everywhere a monetary phenomenon." The quantity theory of money suggests that if the velocity of money is relatively stable — which has not been the case in the US since 2000 — and money is neutral in the long run, i.e., cannot affect real output in the long run, then changes in the money supply greater than real growth will lead to higher prices. Indeed, there is empirical evidence that supports the strong correlation between inflation and money growth in excess of economic growth.

Those familiar with the experience of Japan will note that Japanese government bonds held by the Bank of Japan have crept up relentlessly to represent a majority of outstanding government bonds, with a corresponding increase in reserve money, but with a distinct lack of inflation. The central bank has consistently undershot its inflation objective for decades.

Similarly, the financial crisis-related quantitative easing in the major developed economies did not drive inflation up either. To square this circle in terms of the quantity theory, declines in the velocity of money have offset the impact of QE on broad money or M2.

How might this time be different? Massive deficits run by the major developed economies during 2020 resulted in huge funding requirements that were substantially met by central banks buying government bonds and other assets. This has been done under the labels of QE and liquidity support. But such purchases of government bonds are observationally equivalent to debt monetization, or printing money; the main difference is the intent of the purchases, namely, monetary easing versus debt financing. Thus, the key difference in QE this time, as compared to the experience of Japan or the financial crisis, is the pace of bond purchases and the extent of broad money growth. That is, credit expansion has accompanied the expansion of the central bank balance sheet. In fact, M2 in the U.S. increased sharply while there was unprecedented annual M2 growth during the pandemic period.[1]

In addition to the size and pace of the increase in reserves and broad money, the Fed is continuing QE and recently made changes to its monetary policy framework to allow inflation to exceed the 2 percent target such that inflation averages 2 percent over an unspecified period. This is a flexible form of average inflation targeting.

The Fed has also signalled that it will allow unemployment to fall until it sees signs of inflation increasing to unwelcome levels, and will maintain supportive policies with a view to narrowing the rich–poor divide, or income inequality, and the racial dimension of unemployment.

22.8.2 US output gap and inflation

We next consider the cyclical view of inflation, where inflation is related to the output gap, which is defined as the difference between actual and potential economic output.

Estimates by the International Monetary Fund suggest that there was a large and persistent output gap between 2009 and 2018, which is associated with lower than 2 percent inflation. History informs us that an economic downturn in the context of a financial crisis can be deeper and more persistent than a normal cyclical downturn, and that's exactly what we saw after the 2008 crisis.

The COVID-19 shock is neither like the financial crisis nor a normal recession; policy responses, both in fiscal and monetary terms, have been

---

[1] Post GFC, the growth in the monetary base growth did not translate into growth in broader money as banks and the private sector de-leveraged and rebuilt balances sheets, but in 2020 we did see both reserve money and M2 expand rapidly, as credit was needed by the private sector to survive and the financial sector was in much better shape to support credit expansion.

unprecedented. The pandemic-induced negative output gap in the US is estimated to be less than half the size of the 2008–09 output gap, and is expected to narrow far more rapidly, according to the IMF. Thus, the output gap could close quickly and, given the fiscal stimulus and the huge increase in household savings, could be pushed well into positive territory in the year or two ahead. The IMF's October 2021 forecasts suggest a US output gap averaging 2.2 percent and inflation averaging 2.7 percent during 2022–26 (US 10-year break even inflation was also 2.7 percent as of 12 November 2021).

22.8.3 Supply-side factors

Some of the pickup in inflation across the world is viewed as transitory, as global supply chains reset after a prolonged and difficult pandemic of shutdowns and restarts in the affected economies. Additionally, food price inflation is mainly due to inward-looking policies prioritizing internal food security as a result of COVID-19.

As countries adjust to a new pandemic equilibrium in the context of a pre-pandemic backdrop of political polarization and nationalism, trade tensions, and deglobalization being intensified, it seems inevitable that input, producer, and consumer price inflation will be part of that equilibrium solution. This will have a negative impact on the rich–poor divide.

Some past trends that supported low inflation, such as globalization, online retailing, and price discovery and the gig economy, may have been largely played out. Some may even go into reverse due to re-shoring and reduced ride- and home-sharing.

As major economies commit to "greening" and carbon neutrality over the coming decades, carbon taxes, cap-and-trade schemes, and shifts away from non-renewable and dirty power generation can be expected to drive up energy prices and feed into overall manufacturing and services costs. Some of these factors, along with asset price inflation, will have a negative impact on the rich–poor divide.

22.8.4 Fiscal drivers of inflation

An already dominant feature of the pre-pandemic world was high and growing overall debt levels in the prevailing low-interest rate environment.

Huge pandemic-related fiscal stimulus programmes mean that public debt to GDP ratios in the major economies have or will reach new post-war highs.

The huge public and private debt overhang suggests the likely "fiscal dominance" of monetary policy, i.e., monetary policy, will be formulated with a view to ensuring the country's solvency over inflation and growth targets.

Low and negative real interest rates — through financial repression and high inflation — were effectively used during and after the two world wars to contain and bring down debt to GDP ratios; they were conducted together with post-WW II fiscal consolidation and high growth, which do not seem to be viable options currently for most major economies. Thus, with the effective lower bound for nominal interest rates becoming more and more binding, we may again see a combination of higher inflation and financial repression to contain debt ratios.

To sum up, we have listed various reasons why we may be at an inflection point for inflation. That said, the inflation outlook remains the 64-trillion-dollar question. So, the "this time could be different" inflation story can happen if:

o   output gaps swing into positive territory, supported by fiscal and monetary policy and pent-up demand;
o   money and credit growth continue to be rapid and well in excess of real growth;
o   monetary policy framework changes by the Fed and other central banks mean inflation is permitted to increase above target, and addressed only reactively rather than proactively (potentially unanchoring inflation expectations); and
o   we return to fiscal dominance of monetary policy.

22.9 Asia Forecasts

In Asia, the Asian Development Bank (ADB) expects inflation to remain stable over the long term, with only some countries in Southeast Asia and South Asia showing inflationary pressures.[2]

---

[2] Visit: Economic Forecasts: September 2021 | Asian Development Bank (adb.org).

The ADB and the World Bank, however, predict that prolonged trade tensions, ageing populations, and the attendant diminishing support ratios, as well as weakness in investment and productivity, will not only cause short-term inflation to become more persistent but also result in the anchoring of higher long-term inflation expectations.

22.10 Investing with Inflation in Mind

Asset prices generally comprise the asset-specific risk premium, the expectation of future interest rates, and the term premium obtained from the term structure of interest rates. Hence, the linkage between asset prices, inflation, and interest rates is fundamental.

Many academics have argued that under certain economic conditions, including lax regulatory policy, and off-balance sheet borrowing or the limits to arbitrage (e.g., via short-sale restrictions), a prolonged low-interest regime can create asset price bubbles.

Indeed, as depicted in Figure 22.4, some financial market naysayers and contrarians argue that the current US stock market is overvalued for

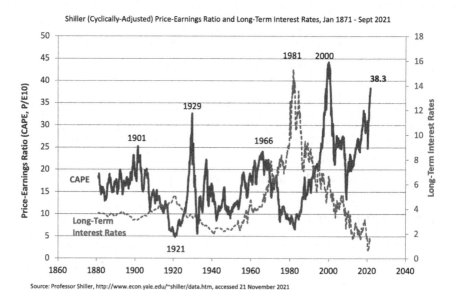

Figure 22.4:   Long-term interest rates and Shiller PE (an indicator of potential bubbles)

this reason, and hence due for a correction if interest rates and inflation were to rise.

We also hope we have demonstrated that, after remaining dormant for several decades, rising inflation could be a more significant risk for investors to contend with going forward. So, what strategies are suitable for investors to explore within this environment?

The fundamental link underpinning all this is the one between asset prices and inflation, the term structure of interest rates, and as a consequence, discount rates, and the asset's associated risk premium.

While the basic mantra to remain diversified to take advantage of the ubiquitous risk/reward trade-offs and efficiencies has not changed, there are perhaps a few asset classes and strategies to emphasize or de-emphasize given the times.

22.10.1 Inflation-protected securities

The first low-hanging fruit strategy is to invest in inflation-protected securities. If the securities are guaranteed by the full faith and credit of a creditworthy and reputable government that issues them, for example, US Treasury Inflation-Protected Securities (TIPS), even better. Such securities hedge against rising inflation, i.e., any decline in the purchasing power of money, and vice versa. And in many cases, including TIPS, the investor is protected against losing the original principal of the bond — if held to maturity — even after a protracted period of deflation.

The current compelling argument against inflation-indexed securities is that, after an extended period of low/negative interest rates, subdued inflation, easy money, QE, etc., these securities are expensive. However, that's like saying one will avoid buying auto insurance for now due to the high accident and insurance premium rates in one's neighbourhood. Anyone with a need to receive $1,000 real dollars safely in 20 years may wish to consider buying 20-year TIPS with the same face value.

22.10.2 High-quality convertibles

While equities and nominal bonds may not in general be what investors flock to during inflationary periods, high-quality convertible bonds potentially could be. In an article published earlier in 2021 Asia Asset Management, one of us proposed convertible bonds as a conservative way in which to participate in volatile equity markets. This includes during inflationary periods.

One reason is that a convertible security has a unique "hockey stick"-like payoff. This makes it resemble a portfolio comprising a call option on equity and a bond. In other words, it provides equity participation in good times and a bond floor when things go sour. This is assuming the investment is in high qualities and the bond doesn't get "busted" due to the issuer going bankrupt.

Another reason is that many convertible bonds are trading cheap based on valuation, i.e., they are trading below their theoretical fair value. For yield-seeking investors, convertibles typically pay coupons at a higher rate than the equity dividend yield, but which are lower than the corresponding straight bonds. Finally, the more uncertain the market or the issuer's underlying equity, the higher the value of the convertible.

22.10.3 Commodities and real estate

Traditionally, commodities and real estate tend to perform well with rising inflation. But we live in different times. Reliance on fossil fuels, which sometimes comprise up to 70 percent of the popular commodity indices, is expected to decline as investors become increasingly conscious about climate. However, non-energy sectors like grains, livestock, and metals may still have some inflation-beating performance characteristics.

Real estate has also been promoted as a hedge against inflation. However, the evidence appears to be mixed. A 2017 study by an MIT economist using NCREIF quarterly data from January 1978 to April 2016 for US office, industrial, apartment, and retail properties found that US retail property income, retail property values, and apartment property values serve as good hedges against inflation.

However, things have changed in the last 5 years with consumers' preference for more convenient online shopping, e-commerce, etc., which was further accelerated by COVID-19 lockdowns, vacancies, and closures on the retail property side. Indeed, Green Street, a real estate analytics and financial market intelligence firm, reported earlier in 2021 that A-rated malls have seen their property values shrink about 45 percent between 2016 and 2020!

In a perverse kind of way, the flood of money leaving the sinking retail property sector may most likely find its way to the residential property sector, especially given humankind's penchant for real assets as a traditional store of value and hedge against inflation, hence lifting prices when one needs them most.

22.11 Conclusion

We may, for all of the reasons discussed, see secular turning points in inflation and interest rates that few asset managers — likely only the baby boomers — have experienced in their careers. The integral link between inflation, interest rates, and asset prices, and the historical implications of such turning points for portfolios, warrants a serious consideration of investment options. Inflation-protected securities, convertibles, and segments of the commodities and real estate may fit the bill.

23

China's Big-Tech Crackdown and Financial Markets: Investors Aren't As Afraid As You Might Think*

23.1 Introduction

The "Big Tech crackdown" by the Chinese government in 2021 to rein in the monopoly power of the nation's leading tech companies sent firms, such as Tencent, Meituan, Pinduoduo, Didi, and New Oriental Education, into a tailspin. The consequences were immediate, with collapsing equity market prices and adverse commentary in the Western media. Do these events foretell doom for foreign investors in China? Do these changes have negative implications for Chinese equities in general? How about the corresponding bond markets? Were they also sending out similar signals?

We believe that the issue is more complicated than many Western commentators have concluded, which we shall discuss in greater detail below. Nevertheless, the evolving scenario requires a nuanced examination of the issues over the long term, particularly given the Chinese bond market's less conspicuous response to the crackdown.

*This chapter is excerpted from the *South China Morning Post,* Print & Online Editions, 10 September 2021. See Cherian and Subrahmanyam (2021).

23.2 Background

China is now the second largest bond market in the world. According to Seafarer, it is a US$15.0 trillion behemoth, second only to the U.S., which is at US$33.9 trillion (as of December 2020). The same report estimates that China's corporate bond market is US$5.3 trillion in size. While the Chinese corporate bond market is still dominated by domestic players, international bond investors' appetite for Chinese bonds is growing, with loosened government regulations, the setup of Bond Connect in July 2017, and greater transparency. For example, the interbank (over-the-counter) bond platform used for trading Chinese bonds, the China Foreign Exchange Trade System (CFETS), which is an arm of the People's Bank of China, i.e., the central bank, mandates the reporting of every bond transaction throughout the day. The CFETS level of data capture is similar to the Financial Industry Regulatory Authority (FINRA)-developed platform called TRACE (Trade Reporting and Compliance Engine), which has been instrumental in facilitating the mandatory reporting of secondary market transactions in the U.S., although the data releases in China are not yet on a tick-by-tick basis.

To complicate matters somewhat, the U.S. administration under Trump — and the associated regulatory authorities — had a data-privacy crackdown on ByteDance's TikTok, Apple, Zoom, and other tech companies, with the U.S. policymakers' concern being how these U.S. firms' data in the U.S. (and China) could be fed back into the data ecosystem built by the Chinese government. In reverse, the Chinese government and its regulatory authorities had similar questions about how Chinese firms' data in the U.S. and China could be captured by U.S. government entities, particularly via the National Security Agency's data surveillance and collection activities. The latter concerns received renewed attention with recent revelations that by using the Pegasus spyware, certain U.S. friendly governments, such as Israel, Saudi Arabia, India, and UAE, were spying on their own citizens and others. Both sides have their respective rallying points, but do they place a damper on foreign investment in China, particularly from U.S. institutions? And what do Chinese capital markets signal about the recent Big Tech crackdown in China?

23.3 The Evidence

To address these questions, we studied the stock market price reaction against the corresponding bond market price reaction to the crackdown. We did so both at the representative stock level and the overall stock/bond index level. The results are indeed revealing. Take the case of Alibaba, the e-commerce firm that rivals Amazon in size, whose American Depositary Receipt (ADR) trades on the NYSE (BABA). The BABA ADR has underperformed the corresponding Alibaba 3.125 percent 28 November 2021 Corporate Bond by a significant margin: $1 invested in the return spread between the two Alibaba-linked securities at the end of 2020 would have yielded $1.61 in the BABA bond's favour by 18 August 2021, as shown in Figure 23.1. In the case of another tech firm, Pinduoduo, China's largest

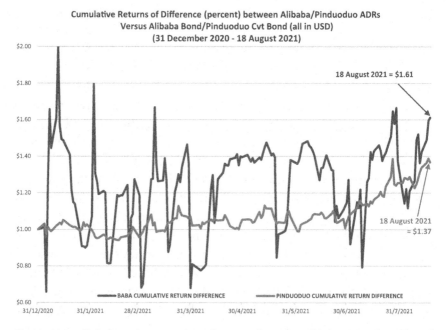

Figure 23.1: Relative price returns performance between Alibaba ADR (NYSE) and Alibaba 3.125 percent 28 November 2021 corporate bond and between Pinduoduo ADR (NASDAQ) and Pinduoduo 1 December 2025 convertible bond (all in USD) over the period 31 December 2020 to 18 August 2021

Source: Bloomberg, Refinitiv.

online grocer, the figure also illustrates that $1 invested in a similar fashion would have yielded $1.37 in the bond's favour by 18 August 2021. The bonds outperformed the stocks handily in both cases.

To make this comparison on a market-wide basis, we plotted the overall performance of three China equity indexes against two Hang Seng Markit iBoxx RMB bond indexes (all in RMB). The CSI 300 Index (SHSZ300) is a market capitalization-weighted index designed to replicate the performance of the top 300 stocks traded on the Shanghai and Shenzhen Stock Exchanges, while the FTSE China A50 (XIN9I) comprises 50 free-float adjusted, liquidity-screened A-share stocks from the same two exchanges that ensure that the index remains representative of the underlying China market. The Hang Seng TECH Index (HSTECH) comprises the 30 largest technology companies listed in Hong Kong, which have high business exposure to technology themes. For bonds, the Hang Seng Markit iBoxx Offshore RMB Bond Overall Index (IBXX001T) and Hang Seng Markit iBoxx Offshore RMB Bond Non-Financials Index (IBXX240T) are designed to reflect the Overall Bond performance and Non-Financials Bond performance of Chinese sovereign and corporate bonds denominated in Chinese Yuan (RMB), respectively, but issued and settled offshore.

Figure 23.2 clearly demonstrates that the bond indexes outperformed their equity index counterparts handsomely over the stated sample period. US$1 invested on 31 December 2020 yielded $0.928 in the SHSZ300, $0.868 in the X1N91, and $0.73807 in the HSTECH, against $1.022 in the IBXX001T and $1.024 in the IBXX240T as of 17 August 2021.

The reasons behind the Chinese government's crackdown on Big Tech firms may be complex, and perhaps mostly justified for the latter's unbridled anti-competitive, data privacy proliferation and perceived negative influence on society — recall, there have been calls to do much the same with large tech firms in the U.S. However, the bond markets in China appear to signal that things are not as bad for investors as the corresponding stock markets or indeed how Western media have made them out to be. Many Chinese commentators are actually cheering their government on, given the widespread disaffection with the tech giants.

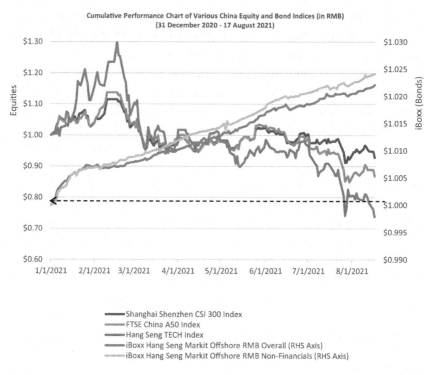

Figure 23.2:   Price returns performance of various China equity and bond indexes (all in RMB) over the period 31 December 2020 to 17 August 2021
Source: Bloomberg, Refinitiv.

23.4 Conclusion

What do these developments imply for investment portfolios? Either the Chinese bond market, unlike its equity counterpart, is grossly inefficient, illiquid, and irrational, or the smart money in Asia appears to be still betting on China, perhaps a little more selectively and in a geopolitically sensitive manner, just as investors in Chinese bonds continue to do. China has never been an easy ride, with its command-and-control form of capitalism, regulatory reforms, and market liberalization policies springing surprises and setbacks on occasion. Despite that caveat, excluding China's capital markets from one's investment strategy is somewhat unimaginable to us.

24

The Swan Song March? An Update on China's Big Tech Crackdown*

24.1 Introduction

The performance of the bond market versus the equities market in the aftermath of China's tech crackdown in 2020 until last year diverged in a curious, significant way. This bifurcation in performance started with the tech companies and subsequently broadened into other sectors. We documented these findings in our **article in the *South China Morning Post* on September 10, 2021**, where we analysed the Chinese government's "Big Tech crackdown" impact on security returns. The government's purported aim was to reduce inequities in wealth across the population, known popularly as seeking to achieve "common prosperity". We showed that a few tech companies and indices, such as Alibaba's bonds and equities, Pinduoduo's bonds and equities, the Hang Seng TECH Equity Index, and the Hang Seng Markit iBoxx Offshore RMB Bond Non-Financials Index, saw bond prices and bond indexes outperforming their equity and equity index counterparts handsomely over the measured sample period, from December 31, 2020 to August 18, 2021.

For example, US$1 invested in the Hang Seng TECH Equity Index and the iBoxx Offshore RMB Bond Non-Financials Index on December 31, 2020 yielded $0.74 and $1.02, respectively, as of August 18, 2021.

---

* This chapter is excerpted from "The Swan Song March? An Update on China's Big Tech Crackdown", *South China Morning Post*, Print & Online Editions, March 25, 2022. See Cherian *et al.* (2022).

Similarly, US$1 invested in the bond/equity return spread between the two Alibaba-linked securities at the end of 2020 yielded $1.61 in the Alibaba bond's favour by August 18, 2021. In the case of Pinduoduo, the return spread yielded $1.37 in the bond's favour over the same period, i.e., the bonds and bond indexes outperformed their equity-related counterparts by a large margin in all cases.

24.2 The Long March in Big Tech

We have since sought to analyse this puzzling dichotomy at a more granular level: We investigated whether investors' beliefs about the series of government measures on the Big Tech companies evolved differently over time. We also examined the effect of the Chinese government's Big Tech crackdown of 2021 on a somewhat larger subset of Chinese tech companies and focused our attention on four key event dates. We conducted a more systematic "event study" on seven large Chinese companies listed on the U.S. Stock Exchanges for which we obtained both equity and bond price data around the four event dates as listed in Table 24.1.

The seven companies we analysed were the main Chinese tech companies: Alibaba (BABA), Meituan (MEITUAN), JD.com (JD), Baidu (BIDU), Hello Group (MOMO), Tencent (TCEHY), and Tencent Music (TME). We ran our analysis on a daily basis over a −20-day to +20-day window around the event date, using the cumulative risk-adjusted performance methodology. The events studied here were chosen to highlight milestones in the history of the Chinese government's crackdown

Table 24.1:   Event Dates of China's "Big Tech Crackdown" in 2021

Event Date	Details
February 7, 2021	The final version of the country's new antitrust guidelines targeting internet platforms took effect on February 7, 2021
March 3, 2021	Chinese regulator SAMR fined 12 companies for "Illegal monopolistic behaviour"
April 10, 2021	SAMR fines Alibaba $2.8 billion for acting like a monopoly
July 24, 2021	China's State Council bans for-profit school tutoring in a sweeping overhaul

through its State Council and the State Administration for Market Regulation (SAMR) over a 6-month period in 2021.

The event study was conducted in four ways:

1. Bond minus Equity cumulative risk-adjusted performance by event date for each stock;
2. Bond minus Equity cumulative risk-adjusted performance across all stocks for each event date;
3. Bond minus Equity cumulative risk-adjusted performance across all event dates for each stock; and
4. Bond minus Equity cumulative risk-adjusted performance across all seven stocks and event dates.

An event study, which is an empirical methodology that is popular in financial literature and typically used to analyse how security returns respond to a particular event, uses cumulative abnormal returns as the measure of outperformance or underperformance. An abnormal return measures the deviation from the security's expected return with respect to the index, while the cumulative abnormal return is the sum of all such abnormal returns over the event window.

Following this convention, we calculated the daily cumulative abnormal returns (CAR) from the spread between bond and equity returns, i.e., the relative performance, for a window of 20 days before and 20 days after each event date. To exclude the possibility of attributing our findings to effects from the overall bond market, we subtracted the returns of a bond market index, the ICE BOFA China Corporate Index (USD), from the returns of the seven bonds. In a similar vein, we subtracted an equity index return, the NASDAQ Composite Index, from the seven equity returns.

The full set of charts for the above four event study scenarios is available in an Internet Appendix. A summary of the key results follows.

Figure 24.1 indicates a highly significant and positive CAR spread, i.e., bonds outperforming stocks, for the various Chinese Internet stocks over each event window, except for the event date February 7, 2021, when the final version of the country's broad antitrust guidelines targeting Internet companies first took effect. All the other three event dates had an effect

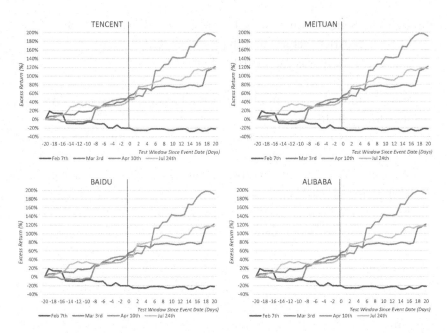

Figure 24.1:   Bond/Equity return spread for tencent (upper left), Meituan (upper right), Baidu (lower left), and Alibaba (lower right) across the four event dates in 2021. Charts depict the bond minus equity cumulative risk-adjusted performance (CAR) spread by event date for each stock

Source: Refinitiv.

on bond versus stock performance, with bonds outperforming stocks in almost all cases.

For example, Tencent showed a CAR spread of close to 180 percent around the event date April 10, 2021, while Alibaba, which bore the brunt of the Chinese regulator SAMR's action, and was fined $2.8 billion for acting like a monopoly, exhibited a CAR spread of about 15 percent only. This was probably because both Alibaba's equity and bonds were severely hit by the SAMR's action. In both cases, however, these CAR spread numbers are too large to be explained by the effect of leverage or other risk factors that are not captured by the methodology at its simplest level.

To examine the effect of the four events across all stocks, we averaged the bond versus stock cumulative risk-adjusted return spread across all stocks and analysed them for each event date. We looked for patterns in

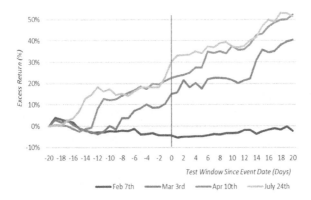

Figure 24.2:   Chinese internet companies' average overall reaction (bond versus equity) on the four event dates in 2021. Chart depicts the bond minus equity cumulative risk-adjusted performance (or CAR) spread averaged across all stocks for each event date
Source: Refinitiv.

the spread over time, that is, if the market had learned anything new with the passage of time about the stringency of the new regime.

One would hence expect the return spread to diminish over these event times as the market gradually absorbs the information associated with the shocks. To the contrary, as Figure 24.2 indicates, the return spread appeared to be close to its highest on April 10, 2021 and July 24, 2021. This is surprising as April 10, 2021 and July 24, 2021 are the last two event dates in our sample period, months after the two previous "crackdowns" on February 7, 2021 and March 3, 2021.

The third event study test is reflected in the left chart of Figure 24.3, in which we examined each Chinese Internet company's overall reaction (bond versus equity CAR spread) averaged across all four event dates in 2021. The graph for Tencent (Tcent) demonstrated the strongest CAR spread (or bonds outperforming stocks) averaged across all the event dates, at around 100 percent, whereas JD.com (JD) appeared to have the weakest relative performance, at around 10 percent.

Finally, the right chart of Figure 24.3 shows the summary effect of China's Big Tech crackdown averaged across all seven Internet platform companies and four event dates. It appears that the CAR spread showed an upward trend on average.

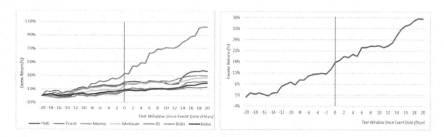

Figure 24.3: Each Chinese internet company's overall reaction (bond versus equity) averaged across all four event dates in 2021. The left chart depicts the bond minus equity cumulative risk-adjusted performance (or CAR) spread averaged across all event dates for each stock. The right chart depicts the same but averaged across all seven stocks and event dates

Source: Refinitiv.

If market participants had updated their prior beliefs about the true intentions of the Chinese government in reining in the Big Tech companies to achieve common prosperity for the nation, they would have expected to see the asymmetric risk-adjusted performance effect on the Chinese bond market versus stock market diminish over the event times. That did not appear to be the case. Therefore, either the bond market investors had been irrational, leading to market inefficiencies, or the crackdown evolved very differently from what was initially announced. Nevertheless, the main participants in the bond markets, mostly institutional investors, had different beliefs from those in the retail-dominated equity market and remained unfazed by the succession of crackdowns.

24.3 Conclusion

As we concluded in the SCMP article of September 2021, the reasons behind the Chinese government's crackdown on the Big Tech companies may be complex and partly due to the widespread discontent with these companies, along with the widening wealth gap in China, which many have attributed to these digital platform companies. That said, the regulatory events in the first 7 months of 2021 indicate that either the Chinese bond market, dominated primarily by institutional firms, as opposed to the retail-heavy equity counterpart, is grossly inefficient, illiquid, and irrational, or the institutional money was still betting on China over that tumultuous 6-month period. This relative performance pattern appears to continue at the index level more recently (November 2021 to early February 2022), although, for individual names, the results are mixed.

Our findings in this study shed light on how market participants reacted to the Chinese government's series of crackdowns on the leading Big Tech companies. It appears that the relative performance between bonds and equities is not easily exploited by arbitrageurs, such as hedge funds, potentially due to market frictions between the bond and equity markets, financial capital moving slowly across the bond and equity markets, and behavioural biases due to differences between bond and equity investors. In other words, there are financial market barriers that prevent investors from exploiting or arbitraging away the performance discrepancy between Chinese bonds and equities through buying one and selling the other.

China remains an enigma for economists and others, vacillating from a country with command-and-control form of free markets to one with unexpected crackdowns of the same markets by both the regulators and the Public Security Bureau on occasion. Notwithstanding this proviso, those believing that they can exclude China's capital markets from the global economy would be naïve. Despite all the media hype, the breadth and depth of the financial markets in the world's second largest economy that has large trade surpluses with the other major economies (e.g., the goods and services trade between the U.S. and China totalled US$658 billion in 2021) mean that global investors have no choice but to look beyond the political rhetoric and continue to tie their fortunes with China.

References

1. Cherian, Joseph and Lassalvy, Laurent, "The role of the state in the pension system." *The Business Times*, 25 October 2011.
2. Lassalvy, Laurent, "Efficient Pension System Design." Working Paper, Center for Asset Management Research & Investments (CAMRI), NUS Business School, 15 July 2011.
3. Merton, Robert C., "On consumption-indexed public pension plans." In *Financial Aspects of the United States Pension System*, edited by Zvi Bodie and John B. Shoven. University of Chicago Press, 1983.
4. Cherian, Joseph and Ong, Shien Jin, "Terms of endurement: Retirement solutions should harness investment science and technology to shockproof plans." *Asia Asset Management,* July 2020, Vol. 25, No. 7. URL: https://www.asiaasset.com/post/23545.
5. Cherian, Joseph and Yan, Emma, "Ring-fencing pensions." *Asia Asset Management*, May 2020a, Vol. 25, No. 5. URL: https://www.asiaasset.com/post/23349.
6. Cherian, Joseph, "Seven pillars of a good retirement savings system." *The Straits Times*, 29 August 2014. URL: https://www.straitstimes.com/opinion/seven-pillars-of-a-good-retirement-savings-system.
7. Cherian, Joseph, "Principles-based MPF: Taking stock." *Asia Asset Management*, December 2020–January 2021, Vol. 25/26, No. 12/1. URL: https://www.asiaasset.com/post/24081.
8. Cherian, Joseph, "If it ain't broke, don't fix it: Just improve it." *Asia Asset Management*, September 2017, Vol. 22, No. 9. URL: http://www.asiaasset.com/aam/2017-09/0917_Pensions.aspx.

9. Cherian, Joseph and Yan, Emma, "In bonds we (still) trust." *Asia Asset Management*, October 2020b, Vol. 25, No. 10. URL: https://www.asiaasset.com/post/23873.

10. Cherian, Joseph and Yan, Emma, "Where are we on the CPF lifetime retirement investment scheme?" *The Business Times*, 14 September 2019a. URL: https://www.businesstimes.com.sg/investing-wealth/where-are-we-on-the-cpf-lifetime-retirement-investment-scheme.

11. Cherian, Joseph and Yan, Emma, "In bonds we (still) trust: Part 2." *Asia Asset Management*, February 2021, Vol. 26, No. 2. URL: https://www.asiaasset.com/post/24244.

12. Cherian, Joseph, "High fees fleece CPF members of investment returns." *The Business Times*, 26 February 2018. URL: https://www.businesstimes.com.sg/opinion/high-fees-fleece-cpf-members-of-investment-returns.

13. Cherian, Joseph, "Asset management fees need to come down." *The Business Standard*, 26 March 2012. URL: https://www.business-standard.com/article/markets/asset-management-fees-need-to-come-down-joseph-cherian-112032600010_1.html.

14. Cherian, Joseph and Yan, Emma, "A time bomb: Low birth rates, longevity put pressure on pension systems." *Asia Asset Management*, November 2019b, Vol. 24, No. 11. URL: https://www.asiaasset.com/post/22839.

15. Cherian, Joseph and Cokeng, Katrina, "Blockchain can democratise access to the best alternatives opportunities." *Asia Asset Management*, September 2019c, Vol. 24, No. 9. URL: https://www.asiaasset.com/post/22670.

16. Cherian, Joseph, "Improving resilience to systemic crises through financing innovations: Lessons and recommendations from Singapore." *Nomura Journal of Asian Capital Markets*, Autumn 2021, Vol. 6, No. 1. URL: https://www.nomurafoundation.or.jp/en/capital/publication_njacm.html.

17. Cherian, Joseph and Chakravarty, Ranjan, "The state of the asset management industry: Tipping points and trends." *Asia Asset Management*, November 2015 (20th Anniversary Special Edition Issue). URL: https://www.asiaasset.com/p/37080.

18. Cherian, Joseph, Kon, Christine, and Weng, William, "A tail of two cities: On the downside risk and loss profile of Asian and North American hedge funds." *The Journal of Alternative Investments*, Summer 2016, Vol. 19, 55–77.

19. Cherian, Joseph, "Seizing the day (seeking relevance in a shrinking sandbox)." *Asia Asset Management*, August 2015a, Vol. 20, No. 8. URL: https://www.asiaasset.com/post/20659-0815-emag. A version of this article also appeared in *The Business Times*, 10 September 2015, entitled "Seeking relevance in a shrinking sandbox."

20. Chakravarty, Ranjan and Cherian, Joseph. "Additional Safeguards for India's Growth Prospects: A Macro-Finance Perspective." Unpublished Working Paper, NUS Business School and Narsee Monjee Institute of Management Studies (NMIMS), June 2014.

21. Cherian, Joseph, "Oh, behave! Why the AIIB can be a win for China and Asia." *NUS Think Business*, 3 July 2015b. A version of this article also appeared in *The Business Times*, 3 July 2015.

22. Cherian, Joseph and Lee, Kang Hoe, "The long march to the future economy." *NUS Think Business*, 22 June 2016. This article also appeared as a series of two essays in *The South China Morning Post* on 11 November 2016 ("To cultivate the industries of the future we need to invest in this intangible human quality") and 12 November 2016 ("Two key steps in the economic march").

23. Cherian, Joseph, "Hazenomics: Facing the fire." *NUS Think Business,* 16 July 2013.

24. Ang, Swee Hoon, Cherian, Joseph, and Loo, Jack, "Hazenomics: Seeing through the smoke." *The Jakarta Post* (20 September 2015). This article also appeared in *The Malaysian Insider* (21 September 2015), and was cited in an INTER PRESS SERVICE (IPS) News Agency feature article entitled "ASEAN agreement on haze? As clear as smoke" (13 October 2015).

25. Cherian, Joseph and Yeung, Bernard, "The state as insurer of last resort." Chapter 11, pp. 71–77. In *Impact of COVID-19 on Asian Economies and Policy Responses,* https://doi.org/10.1142/12072, edited by Sumit Agarwal, Zhiguo He, and Bernard Yeung, https://doi.org/10.1142/9789811229381_0011, World Scientific, January 2021.

26. Cherian, Joseph, "Financial tradeoffs matter during pandemics." *Asia Asset Management*, 14 April 2020. URL: https://www.asiaasset.com/post/23280-financial-tradeoffs-0409.

27. Cherian, Joseph and Khatri, Yougesh, "A turning point? (After decades of declines, inflation and interest rates may be on the uptrend)." *Asia Asset Management*, 25th Anniversary Special Edition Issue, November–December 2021. URL: www.asiaasset.com/post/25350.

28. Chakravarty, Ranjan, Cherian, Joseph, Nishimura, Kiyoshi, and Wong, Heang Fine, "Making infrastructure assets more palatable." *Asia Asset Management*, May 2018, Vol. 23, No. 5. URL: https://www.asiaasset.com/post/21575-0518-ra.

29. Cherian, Joseph and Subrahmanyam, Marti, "China's Big-Tech crackdown and financial markets: Investors aren't as afraid as you might think."

South China Morning Post, Print & Online Editions, 10 September 2021. URL: https://www.scmp.com/week-asia/opinion/article/3148098/chinas-crackdown-big-tech-firms-isnt-scaring-away-bond-investors.

Cherian, Joseph, Mo, Jingyuan, Subrahmanyam, Marti, and Xiao, Tingyi, "The swan song march? An update on China's Big Tech crackdown." *South China Morning Post,* Print & Online Editions, 25 March 2022. URL: https://www.scmp.com/week-asia/opinion/article/3171760/swan-song-march-update-chinas-big-tech-crackdown.

30. Cherian, Joseph and Sansi, Manish, "Algo's got rhythm." *Asia Asset Management,* December 2019–January 2020, Vol. 24/25, No. 12/1. URL: https://www.asiaasset.com/post/22929.

31. Cherian, Joseph, Kon, Christine, and Li, Ziyun, "Are hedge funds just traditional beta?" *Asia Asset Management,* April 2020, Vol. 25, No. 4. URL: https://www.asiaasset.com/post/23251.

32. Cherian, Joseph and Yong, Danny, "The Central Provident Fund (CPF): Making a good programme even better." *NUS Lee Kuan Yew School of Public Policy IPS Commons,* Saturday, 16 August 2014. URL: https://ipscommons.sg/making-a-good-programme-even-better/.

Printed in the United States
by Baker & Taylor Publisher Services